STEVEN J. LAWSON
PHILIPPIANS FOR YOU

thegoodbook
COMPANY

Philippians For You
© Steven J. Lawson, 2017. Reprinted 2018.

Published by:
The Good Book Company

Tel (US): 866 244 2165
Tel (UK): 0333 123 0880
Email (US): info@thegoodbook.com
Email (UK): info@thegoodbook.co.uk

Websites:

North America: www.thegoodbook.com
UK: www.thegoodbook.co.uk
Australia: www.thegoodbook.com.au
New Zealand: www.thegoodbook.co.nz

(Hardcover) ISBN: 9781784981150
(Paperback) ISBN: 9781784981143

Design by André Parker

Printed in India

CONTENTS

SERIES PREFACE

Each volume of the *God's Word For You* series takes you to the heart of a book of the Bible, and applies its truths to your heart.

The central aim of each title is to be:
- Bible centered
- Christ glorifying
- Relevantly applied
- Easily readable

You can use *Philippians For You:*

To read. You can simply read from cover to cover, as a book that explains and explores the themes, encouragements and challenges of this part of Scripture.

To feed. You can work through this book as part of your own personal regular devotions, or use it alongside a sermon or Bible-study series at your church. Each chapter is divided into two (or occasionally three) shorter sections, with questions for reflection at the end of each.

To lead. You can use this as a resource to help you teach God's word to others, both in small-group and whole-church settings. You'll find tricky verses or concepts explained using ordinary language, and helpful themes and illustrations along with suggested applications.

These books are not commentaries. They assume no understanding of the original Bible languages, nor a high level of biblical knowledge. Verse references are marked in **bold** so that you can refer to them easily. Any words that are used rarely or differently in everyday language outside the church are marked in gray when they first appear, and are explained in a glossary towards the back. There, you'll also find details of resources you can use alongside this one, in both personal and church life.

Our prayer is that as you read, you'll be struck not by the contents of this book, but by the book it's helping you open up; and that you'll praise not the author of this book, but the One he is pointing you to.

Carl Laferton, Series Editor

Bible translations used:

- NASB: New American Standard Bible (this is the Bible version being quoted unless otherwise stated

- ESV: English Standard Version

Philippians is the sunniest of Paul's epistles. Its dominant theme is joy. Notes of joy sound through the epistle from beginning to end, and the theme reaches its pinnacle with a triumphant double imperative in Philippians 4:4: "Rejoice in the Lord always; again I will say, rejoice!"

What makes this so remarkable is that Philippians is one of Paul's prison epistles. He wrote it while being held in chains, nearly forgotten in a sluggish legal system, awaiting a trial to determine whether he would live or die. He makes repeated mention of his imprisonment (1:7, 13, 14, 17). He speaks of the imperial guard who were assigned to keep him confined (v 13). He ponders what the life-or-death verdict might mean (v 21-24).

The biblical record itself strongly suggests that Philippians was written from Rome during the first of Paul's two imprisonments there. In his closing words, the apostle mentions fellow believers who were members of Caesar's household. That would be out of place anywhere besides Rome. And the details given in the epistle itself harmonize perfectly with Luke's words in the final verses of the book of Acts. There we learn that Paul was held in Rome under house arrest, most likely chained constantly to a Roman guard, for "two whole years at his own expense, and welcomed all who came to him, proclaiming the kingdom of God and teaching about the Lord Jesus Christ with all boldness and without hindrance" (Acts 28:30-31, ESV).

Although Paul was therefore able (on a diminished scale) to carry out the ministry he was called to, this arrangement was neither convenient nor pleasant for him. His arrival in Rome had come at the end of a four-and-a-half-year ordeal that started in Jerusalem with his arrest on false charges (Acts 21:27-36). On the journey to Rome, he was beaten, shipwrecked, snake-bitten, denied ample food and water, subjected to harsh conditions and cruel treatment, and otherwise inconvenienced in countless ways. The travelogue he gives in 2 Corinthians 11:24-28 is dominated by the various afflictions he suffered on that harrowing journey to Rome:

"Five times I received at the hands of the Jews the forty lashes less one. Three times I was beaten with rods. Once I was stoned. Three times I was shipwrecked; a night and a day I was adrift at sea; on frequent journeys, in danger from rivers, danger from robbers, danger from my own people, danger from Gentiles, danger in the city, danger in the wilderness, danger at sea, danger from false brothers; in toil and hardship, through many a sleepless night, in hunger and thirst, often without food, in cold and exposure. And, apart from other things, there is the daily pressure on me of my anxiety for all the churches." (ESV)

Hard as it is to conceive, there were Christians in and around Rome who became so jealous of Paul's influence and his giftedness that they set themselves up as his rivals, hoping their preaching would add to his afflictions (Philippians 1:17).

This no doubt was mainly because Paul was a political hot potato. His notoriety, together with his undaunted boldness, made it costly to be perceived as his friend or companion. As a result, he began to lose the support of many friends and former companions. Some, like Demas, fell in love with this present world, and deserted the apostle because of the hardships that came with being his companion (2 Timothy 4:10). By the time he wrote Philippians, Paul could say, "I have no one like [Timothy], who will be genuinely concerned for your welfare. For they all seek their own interests, not those of Jesus Christ" (Philippians 2:20-21, ESV). A few years later, near the end of his life, Paul would write to his closest protégé, "You are aware that all who are in Asia turned away from me" (2 Timothy 1:15, ESV). No leading figure in all of church history has ever had more reason than the apostle Paul to be downcast and discouraged.

And yet, as he makes clear in this epistle to the church at Philippi, Paul's mind and heart were full of rejoicing—a resounding joy that was utterly impervious to any circumstance. Therefore Paul's gladness simply overwhelms whatever pathos we might expect to dominate an epistle penned from prison. It's a joy that is real and heartfelt, deep and palpable.

Our age has given us a plethora of amenities and conveniences that Paul could never have even imagined. Yet our daily lives are fast-paced, hectic, and full of trouble and stress. Real joy is a rare commodity in civilized Western culture. Sadly, even most of the visible church is hardly a bastion of genuine joy. We desperately need the message Paul gave the church at Philippi.

I am constantly drawn to this epistle because every time I read it, Paul's passionate sense of joy stirs my heart. I love preaching from Philippians because its message is the perfect remedy for the somber mood that often dominates these troubled times in which we live.

There are, of course, notes of rebuke, correction, and urgent warning in Philippians, but Paul always returns to the message of joy. So the epistle runs the gamut of human passions, but always finds resolution by returning to the keynote of joy. It is both astonishing and personally inspiring that such indefatigable joy dominated the heart, mind, and teaching of the apostle Paul even after all those years of suffering. This attribute looms large in his character, and it helps explain his unflagging faithfulness, his far-reaching influence, and his remarkable resilience. That joy is infectious, too.

This commentary on Philippians is a real treasure. No one surpasses Steve Lawson's ability to distill rich truths from the text of Scripture and communicate them with eloquent clarity and warm affection. In fact, Steve's preaching, like Paul's epistles, is full of contagious passion. His writing is notable for its compelling readability. His insights are profound and eye-opening. You will be edified and encouraged. You'll gain much in your understanding of this wonderful epistle and the apostle who wrote it.

John MacArthur, November 2016

To Eric Lindsay,

A servant and supporter of pastors and spiritual leaders around the world.

I am grateful to be one of those men. He is a true friend and "Barnabas" to me.

INTRODUCTION TO PHILIPPIANS

When a pastor preaches his last series for the church where he has served as pastor, the Scripture he chooses should be carefully selected, to leave a lasting impact with positive encouragement upon the lives of his precious flock. This is where I found myself recently as I came to the end of my twelve-year pastorate at Christ Fellowship Baptist Church in Mobile, Alabama, where I had been founding pastor.

I chose the book of Philippians.

This would be my final deposit in the hearts of those wonderful believers who had become very dear to me. For many of them, I had been their pastor for two decades, with many coming to faith in Christ under my pastorate.

So why did I select the book of Philippians to preach as my final pulpit series? And why should the book of Philippians be so important to your spiritual life? Here are seven reasons.

First, this is an *intensely personal* book. The relationship that the apostle Paul had developed with the believers in Philippi was a close bond marked by a deep affection. Paul was the founding pastor of this church, and had already invested much of his life in them. He warmly refers to them as "my joy and crown" (4:1). This book reveals the depth of authentic Christian fellowship between believers. This kind of love is what I sought to convey to my flock. Likewise, this is what you need to experience in your spiritual life. Your walk with the Lord will thrive to the extent that you are a part of the kind of community that the Philippian church and their founding pastor enjoyed together.

Second, the book of Philippians is a *joy-producing* book. It was written by Paul to encourage the hearts of believers and urge them to rejoice in the Lord (2:18; 3:1; 4:4). Joy is a spiritual grace that we all need to experience in our Christian lives. We live in a world of stress and anxiety that all too easily and subtly can steal the peace of God from our hearts. We need an abundant, overflowing joy to flood our souls. The book of Philippians is written for that very purpose—to point us to that joy. Surely, there is not a one of us who does not need to know more of the supernatural joy of the Lord in our lives.

Third, the book of Philippians is a *gospel-focused* book. There is a repeated emphasis upon the good news of salvation that is in God's Son, Jesus Christ (1:5, 7, 12, 16, 27; 2:22; 4:3, 15). Paul places great stress upon the saving message of the gospel, as well as the need for us to live it out in our daily lives. This is what Paul continuously mentioned in order to encourage the believers in Philippi. They needed a gospel focus. We are no different.

Fourth, the book of Philippians is a *doctrinally-rich* book. It is an apostolic letter that contains great theological truth. Found in this book is the signature passage on the self-emptying of Christ in his incarnation. Here Paul teaches how the Son of God entered into this world to take upon himself human flesh and die for sins (2:6-8). Further, we see the exaltation of Christ to the right hand of God the Father (2:9-11). We discover the eternal security of the believer (1:6). The list could go on. These are truths that must be ever at the forefront of the mind of each believer, including you and me, and they are doctrines taught in the letter to the Philippians.

Fifth, the book of Philippians is a *prayer-inclining* book. From the opening of this book, the apostle Paul expresses his sincere prayers offered on behalf of the Philippians (1:3-11). In the last chapter of this letter, Paul reminds the believers once again of the need to cast their burdens upon the Lord in order to experience his peace (4:6-7). In like manner, we should read the book of Philippians and allow it to deepen our own prayer life. Not a one of us is without need of further instruction and encouragement in regards to coming before the Lord in fervent, frequent, believing prayer.

Sixth, the book of Philippians is a *holiness-growing* book. This letter teaches us much about how to live the Christian life. Paul will tell us that we bear great responsibility to work out our salvation in fear and trembling (2:12-13). At the same time, he will instruct us that it is God who is at work within us for his good pleasure. We will find ourselves challenged to forget what lies behind, and press forward to the upward call of God in Christ Jesus. This teaching on spiritual growth is applicable for the life of every Christian. Expect to grow in a desire for holiness and a life of holiness as we walk through this letter.

Seventh, the book of Philippians is an *eternity-gazing* book. Here we are given the eternal perspective we need as we are faced with life's difficulties (3:20-21). In the opening chapter, Paul expresses his confidence that the work of God is going forward despite the fact that there are other believers in Rome jealous of his ministry (1:12-14). This letter reminds us that we must rejoice whenever the gospel is advancing, regardless of the personal affliction we might have to suffer. Based on Paul's tone as he writes this letter, we would never guess that he is actually writing from a prison cell. The apostle personally models how to live triumphantly and joyfully in the midst of difficult circumstances.

So as we study the book of Philippians together in this expository guide, we should expect to experience a greater realization of the fullness of God in Jesus Christ for our lives. This is a remarkable book that, I trust, will leave a lasting effect upon your life. May the Lord use the pages that follow to lead you into a deeper realization of the grace of the Lord Jesus Christ.

1. A PERSONAL LETTER

Can you imagine receiving a handwritten letter from the **apostle***
Paul addressed to you personally? How excited you would be to receive a piece of inspired writing from the leading spiritual teacher
of the day. That is precisely what the early believers in Philippi must
have felt when this correspondence was delivered to them. There
was Paul's name on the **epistle***—and their name right beside it!
We can count on both hands the number of churches in history that
have been so privileged—and the Philippians church was one such
body of believers.

Yet in a broader sense, every authentic church in every generation
has been so privileged. Far more than this being merely an ancient
letter, this letter is intended for every church and every Christian in
every generation. In this letter, God himself is still speaking to each
one of us today. Though this letter was written two thousand years
ago to the church at Philippi, it finds itself in the Bible for our spiritual good and growth, preserved for you and me and our benefit
as well. This epistle is for you and me even today. As we begin this
study of the book of Philippians, it is my prayer that there will be
ignited within your heart a growing closeness to the Lord, and a new
joy in him. In this chapter, we will consider together the first two
verses of this highly personal epistle, which form the opening section
known as a salutation.

---

* Words in **gray** are defined in the Glossary (page 231).

The Servants

In the very first word of this letter, Paul begins by identifying himself as its author (**v 1a**[*]). It was typical in the first century for the writer of a piece of correspondence to record his name first rather than placing it at the end as is our custom today. In inscribing his name first, Paul is not being self-centered. Rather, he is simply letting the Philippians know that this letter is from him, a common practice of the day.

"Paul" is the Roman or Greek name of this towering figure, who was previously called by his Hebrew name, "Saul." Many would insist that the apostle Paul was the greatest Christian who ever lived. He was so active for the Lord that it could well be said he lived the life of nine men. He was a dynamic missionary, church planter, powerful preacher, caring pastor, gifted **evangelist**, astute **theologian**, brilliant teacher, **itinerant** speaker, and prolific author—all merged into one extraordinary person. This is the same Paul who authored thirteen epistles in the New Testament. It was something special to receive this letter from the chief apostle in the church.

In **verse 1**, Paul states that he is accompanied by "Timothy," his young co-worker, about whom we will discover more when we reach the second half of Philippians 2. Timothy served Paul on many levels as his travel assistant, trusted companion, and constant supporter. The apostle was the primary human instrument in the spiritual development of this younger man. Similarly, every one of us needs to have a Timothy in our life. We all need someone who is a partner with us in serving God. It may be a prayer partner or a personal encourager. It may be a spouse, an old friend, or an older mentor. It may be a teaching assistant. Whoever this person may be in your life, there is great blessing in pursuing this kind of relationship—a trusted associate like Timothy in serving the Lord. "Two are better than one" (Ecclesiastes 4:9).

Both Paul and Timothy are identified as "bond-servants of Christ Jesus" (Philippians **1:1**). At the outset of his other letters, Paul often

---

[*] All Philippians verse references being looked at in each part of the chapter are in **bold**.

refers to himself as "an apostle" of Christ Jesus (Romans 1:1; 1 Corinthians 1:1; 2 Corinthians 1:1; Galatians 1:1; Ephesians 1:1; Colossians 1:1; 2 Timothy 1:1; Titus 1:1). Paul certainly held such a position of spiritual authority in the early church. But with the Philippians, there appears to be no need for him to remind them of this elevated credential. Presumably, they are already mindful and respectful of his lofty spiritual responsibility. Instead, the emphasis he chooses to make is relational and personal. He humbles himself and stresses his commitment to serve them. This serves as a great reminder that all authentic leadership in the church must be servant-leadership.

The word Paul uses is "bond-servant" (*doulos* in the original Greek), which actually means "slave." A slave is assigned an even lower position than a servant. In the first century, a servant would have owned a few possessions and have been protected by certain rights. He would have been hired for a certain project and then was able to return home to his normal life. But this was not the case with a slave. A slave actually belonged to his master like a piece of property. He did not have a life of his own. Further, a slave did not own anything. He was entirely dependent upon his master to meet all his needs. Neither could he travel anywhere without his master's consent. His entire life existed to please his owner.

The point here is that "bond-servant" is precisely how Paul saw himself. And so, this is how he presented himself to the Philippians—as a slave-leader: a slave of Christ who had been bought by his master to be his possession. Of course, to serve such a master—the Master who died out of love for his "bond-servants"—is neither restrictive nor an imposition. It is a privilege and a joy, for the great **paradox** is that such slavery brings true freedom—freedom from fear, futility and death. The chief aim of Paul's whole life was to please the Lord Jesus Christ. This humble-yet-wonderful position is not restricted to Paul and Timothy. Every believer in Christ is designated as his slave. In other passages, we are identified as joint heirs with Christ and children of the King. But here we are designated to be his slaves. As the slaves of Christ, we belong to him and exist to serve and glorify him. To be sure, no slave ever had a more benevolent Master than do we. He freely provides every **grace** we need to live abundantly. But our Master he is.

This self-identification is how Paul humbly opens this letter. He reveals himself and his son in the faith, Timothy, as slaves. No author ever began his correspondence by assuming a more lowly posture. This is the **meekness** of mind which each one of us must assume. In being chosen to serve the Lord, we have a high calling to a lowly position.

The Saints

Paul next designates to whom he is writing: "all the saints in Christ Jesus who are at Philippi" (Philippians **1:1b**). This identifies all the believers as "saints in Christ Jesus." Every genuine Christian is a "saint," which means "a holy one." The words "holy," "hallowed," "saint," and "**sanctification**" all come from the same Greek root. These four words sound different in our English language, but they are similar in the Greek language. "Saint" is the most common word Paul uses to address believers in the early church. With this understanding, this phrase could be translated as "to all the holy ones in Christ Jesus who are at Philippi."

The word "saint" is drawn from the word "holy" (*hagios* in the Greek), which refers to one who is set apart from the moral pollution of this world and set apart unto God. To be a saint means that by the operation of grace, a Christian no longer lives a life of pursuing sin in the evil world system and, instead, is pursuing moral purity. This involves both a negative and a positive separation. This is the dramatic change that takes place in every believer's life when they are converted to Christ. They are immediately set apart by God from their old life of sin, negatively, and are engaged to a new life of purity, positively.

As saints in their historical time and geographical place, these Christians stood out in the corrupt world of the Roman Empire like bright stars on a dark night (2:15-16). They were easily distinguished as they lived in an unholy culture. These believers were traveling a different path and headed in a different direction than the immoral society around them. They had a radically different standard of morality that produced an entirely different lifestyle. Everything about them was different from the polluted world in which they lived. Their families were different, their businesses were different, and their conversations were different.

At the same time, Paul stresses that every believer in Philippi was, **positionally**, "in Christ Jesus." Before their conversion, they belonged to the evil world system with its anti-God agenda. But they had been delivered out of the kingdom of darkness and brought into vital union and communion with Christ Jesus. They were washed in his blood and given a new standing in his grace. They were made citizens of the kingdom of God. This little **prepositional** phrase, "in Christ Jesus," makes all the difference to everything.

> Being in Christ Jesus makes all the difference to everything.

The same is true for all believers in Jesus Christ. We, too, are vitally connected to Christ and have entered into a personal relationship with him. The fullness of his all-sufficient life is flowing into our lives. Grace upon grace is being multiplied in our souls. All that Christ is and all that he possesses belongs to us. Being in Christ Jesus makes all the difference to everything. And so Paul begins this letter by reminding his first readers, and Christians through the ages, that they have this privileged position in Christ Jesus. As the late British theologian Alec Motyer wrote:

> "The exclusive place which the Lord Jesus Christ occupies in relation to the Christian has three aspects, which Paul indicates here by the words in, of, and from: a saint in Christ Jesus, a servant of Christ Jesus, and grace and peace from ... the Lord Jesus Christ." (*The Message of Philippians*, page 26)

The Setting

Paul next identifies the geographical location of these "saints" as being "in Philippi" (**1:1b**). In the first century, this ancient city was in eastern Macedonia, which is modern northeastern Greece. As a Roman colony, it enjoyed a different political status from the typical city in that day. Philippi had a close identification with Rome, so much so that it was called "Little Rome."

"As such it was a Rome in miniature, a reproduction on a small scale of the imperial city."

(William Hendriksen, *Philippians,* page 6)

The citizens enjoyed full Roman citizenship with many special privileges. They were exempt from paying the heavy taxes that citizens in other cities paid. They were excused from certain military service. They also received bolstered military protection because Philippi was an outpost for Roman soldiers.

As a thriving Roman city, Philippi enjoyed the stunning beauty of Roman architecture. The people proudly wore the Roman style of clothing. They spoke Latin, the language of educated cultured citizens, rather than Greek, which was so prevalent within the empire. Proud of its connection with Rome, Philippi boasted of its status as a colony of the empire.

Even so, when on his second missionary journey Paul had visited Philippi and preached the **gospel** (Acts 16:14-34), God opened the heart of a woman named Lydia, who was converted to Christ along with others. Paul's powerful preaching, along with the liberation of the demon-possessed slave girl and the ensuing loss of income for her master, created a riot which caused him to be arrested, beaten and thrown into prison. But Paul kept preaching. At midnight, God sent a powerful earthquake that led to the conversion of the Philippian jailer and his entire household. In the aftermath, a church was spontaneously birthed, the church to which Paul now writes this letter. This dramatic beginning produced a tight bond between Paul and the Philippians.

Here we see the importance of the local church. If you are a believer in Jesus Christ, you should be an active member of a local church wherever you live. Christianity was never intended to be lived in isolation from other believers. God's design for healthy spiritual living is for us to be a functioning part of a church where the word is preached.

Questions for reflection

1. "In this letter, God himself is still speaking to each one of us today." How does this affect how you will approach your time reading the letter to the Philippians?

2. Given who Christ is, why is it a privilege, rather than oppressive, to be one of his "bond-servants"?

3. How are you, as a "saint," living a set-apart life in your particular place and time, in what you pursue and what you refrain from?

PART TWO

The Shepherds

As Paul continues his introduction to his letter, he recognizes the leadership of the church. He singles out two groups who serve the needs of the congregation. These are "the overseers and deacons" of the church (Philippians **1:1c**). The "overseers" are identified elsewhere in Scripture as "elders" (e.g. Titus 1:5), who shepherd the flock of God. The word "overseer" indicates the spiritual oversight and management they are to give to the church. The term "elder" speaks of the spiritual maturity required to be a spiritual leader in the church (1 Timothy 3:1-7; Titus 1:5-9). In order for someone to be an effective overseer, there must be spiritual growth in his own personal walk with the Lord. This advancement in grace must be evident in his life if he is to serve in this capacity.

By mentioning the "overseers," Paul intends to elevate the importance of these spiritual leaders in the church. At the outset of this epistle, he is intentionally drawing the focus of the whole congregation to these men. Paul desires that they be esteemed, supported, and followed in the direction they provide. He calls them "overseers" to remind the flock of the strategic responsibility they have. Concerning the role of overseers, John MacArthur explains:

"They mediate the rule of Christ in local churches by preaching, teaching, setting godly examples, and giving Spirit-guided leadership." (*The MacArthur New Testament Commentary on Philippians*, page 16)

Serving alongside the overseers are the "deacons." The word "deacon" means "servant." In the first century, it was used of one who ministered meals at a table. As those called alongside the overseers, deacons are crucial to the spiritual health of any local church. While they do not have the same responsibility as the elders, they nevertheless are vital in the care of people and in implementing the ministries of the church. Those who served as deacons facilitated **ministry** behind the scenes. They especially cared for the widows and met many physical needs (see Acts 6:1-7). These servants were involved in the lives of people at a practical level. They were special instruments who executed what the overseers perceived to be the ministry focuses of the church.

This passage reminds us of the enormous stewardship that the Lord has entrusted to the overseers and deacons. No church can rise any higher than the godliness of its leaders. Like produces like. Like pastor, like people. Spiritually mature overseers exert a spiritual influence upon those they lead. They are charged by God to chart the course for the church. Humble deacons are to help in carrying out this vision and in implementing its strategies. As the church is served by overseers and deacons, there is a sense of security for its members. You can never pray too much for those who serve your church as overseers and deacons.

The Salutations

Paul continues his introduction with the familiar greeting, "Grace to you and peace from God our Father and the Lord Jesus Christ" (Philippians **1:2**). He could desire and request nothing greater for the church at Philippi than that they would enjoy "grace" and "peace." Requesting grace and peace was a common way in the first century of greeting others upon entering a house. G. Walter Hansen explains:

> "Grace is Paul's adaptation of the 'greetings' at the beginning of Greek letters of his day. Peace echoes the common Jewish greeting (Shalom). Paul's combination of the Greek and Jewish greetings reflections the intersection of Greek and Jewish cultures in Paul's expressions." (*The Letter to the Philippians,* page 43)

Here, though, Paul gives the greeting a distinctively Christian meaning by adding, "from God our Father and the Lord Jesus Christ." In other words, all grace and all peace comes from the entire **Godhead**.

The first of these words, "grace," is the very heart of the Christian message. Grace summarizes the gospel. When Paul asks for grace, he is not asking that they would receive saving grace. He has stated in **verse 1** that they are "saints in Christ Jesus." They are already reconciled to God through their faith in the saving work of Christ upon the cross. They have already been made spiritually alive by the Holy Spirit and brought into living union with Christ. There is nothing that could make them any more a saint than they already are. So "grace to you" is a request that they enter into a fuller experience of grace in their Christian lives. It is a request for daily grace that will enable them to live in a manner that honors God—that they would know the all-sufficient grace of God in their lives.

To put it another way, Paul is saying, *May the fullness of the Holy Spirit be upon you.* This **benediction** is echoed in the last verse of this epistle. Paul will conclude his letter, "The grace of the Lord Jesus Christ be with your spirit" (4:23). These two requests form bookends around the entire book. This epistle ends as it starts, with this request for grace in Christian living. When Paul requests that this grace be "with your spirit," he is asking that it be operative in the very depth of their souls. He is asking that this God-given power be in the core of their innermost beings.

Paul also asks that the "peace" of God be with them (**1:2**). This is *not* referring to peace *with* God, which is **objective** peace with God given to those who trust in Christ because Jesus has borne our punishment of rebellion against God, in our place, once for all, in his death. "Being justified by faith, we have peace with God" (Romans 5:1). At the moment of conversion, all believers in Christ enter into a state of peace with God. Previous to their **new birth**, the Philippians were enemies of God. But now they have become accepted friends, who are at peace with God.

The peace that Paul is talking about here in Philippians **1:2** is the **subjective** peace *of* God. Notice how he words this as "peace from God," rather than peace with God. He means the personal experience of supernatural peace within their souls. Only God can give this inner tranquility. This is the quiet calm within the human spirit in the midst of life's raging storms. This personal serenity comes from knowing that God is in control of all circumstances, and causes all things to work together for our good so that we might become more and more like Christ (Romans 8:28-30). No challenge that a believer can ever face will be independent of the sovereign control of God over their circumstances.

The relationship between grace and peace is important. There is no peace until there first is grace. That is why Paul mentions grace first. Wherever there is grace, peace inevitably results. The grace of God in a life prepares the way for the peace of God to flood a heart. Grace is the root, and peace is the fruit. Put another way, grace is the cause, and peace is the result. These two spiritual blessings are like twins. Wherever you see grace, there you will find peace.

The Source

All grace and peace come "from God our Father and the Lord Jesus Christ" (Philippians **1:2**). There is no grace apart from God the Father through the Lord Jesus Christ. Neither is there any peace within the heart outside of knowing God through Jesus Christ. This is a theme Paul will return to through the letter, and especially in 4:6-9. We must know God by trusting Christ in order to experience grace and peace through the Spirit. The Bible says that God is the God of all peace (2 Corinthians 1:3). There is no grace or peace outside of knowing him.

Notice the dual source of grace and peace. These blessings come from both God the Father and God the Son. There is an ever-flowing fountain of grace and peace that comes streaming into every believer in fullest measure. It is, in essence, all-sufficient grace and all-sustaining peace that is flooding into our lives and swelling its banks.

Further, notice that Paul is teaching that the fullness of **deity** is shared equally by the Father and the Son. Grace and peace come from God our Father and the Lord Jesus Christ. This fact stresses the co-equality of God the Father and his Son. These two Persons within the Trinity possess the same divine essence and attributes. So this verse makes a clear statement affirming the full deity of Jesus Christ. It places Jesus Christ on equal footing with God the Father. Currently, the Lord Jesus Christ is seated at the right hand of the Father and occupies the place of all authority in heaven and earth. Jesus is submissive to the Father in his role within the Godhead, but he yields as an equal.

Here is the all-sufficient grace of God for Christian living. Here is the abundance of divine peace for our often troubled souls. We will never face a trial beyond what the grace and peace of God enables us to endure. Contained in this greeting is the promised abundant supply of God to meet all our needs in troubled times. Our greatest difficulties can never exhaust the unlimited resources of God. There is far more grace and abundant peace to sustain, strengthen, and secure us than we can ever need.

> Our greatest difficulties can never exhaust the unlimited resources of God.

The experience of this grace and peace does not happen automatically. It is incumbent upon every believer to avail themselves of the **means of grace**. That is to say, we must read and study the word of God. We must internalize and implement its truths. We must set our minds on things above, not on things of the earth. We must worship God before his throne of grace. We must pray and cast our burdens upon him. We must live in close fellowship with other believers. We must serve one another as we carry out our Christian duties. As we do, God abundantly supplies his grace and peace to our souls.

It is impossible to imagine a more positive beginning to any letter than the way this one begins. It is wonderful to know that its truths apply to us, if we are in Christ Jesus. And it prepares us to learn more and experience more of the fullness of what God has prepared for us as his people through the rest of this hope-filled, joy-soaked letter.

Questions for reflection

1. "You can never pray too much for those who serve your church as overseers and deacons." Does this thought need to change the priorities in your prayers?

2. What difference will "grace to you" and "peace from God" make to your day today, and tomorrow?

3. Are there other places you are tempted to look to for your peace? How does the result of locating your sense of peace there compare to when you seek it in God?

2. THICK SKIN, TENDER HEART

Ministry inevitably brings conflict. Whatever ministry you are involved in, if there is no resistance to your work, it is because there has been no movement forward. In the face of such confrontation, everyone who is in ministry (whether a pastor, or an elder, or a children's leader, and so on) must be a resilient figure. They must possess thick skin that enables them to deflect the opposition that rises up against them. And they must have a hard outer shell if they are to fulfill the work God has given them to do.

However, in the midst of these challenges, all who serve must also have a loving heart toward people. Maintaining this delicate balance between toughness and tenderness is the challenge for anyone in Christian ministry of some kind. We must be strong in purpose while being sensitive toward people. These two virtues must be **mutually inclusive**.

This rare combination of a thick skin and a tender heart was clearly seen in the life of the apostle Paul. Amid the demands of his challenging work, it is this virtue of loving people that bleeds from his heart. As he writes to the church at Philippi, we discern the profile of this pastor's heart. Ten years prior to writing this letter, the apostle Paul first came to Philippi while on his second missionary journey. He proclaimed the gospel of Christ, and many souls were converted; and from that miraculous work, a church was spontaneously birthed. Through this exhilarating experience, a permanent bond of affection was established in his heart for this church. Paul would plant other churches, but there remained a special affinity in his heart for this group of believers. A decade later, while imprisoned in Rome, the apostle writes this letter to the Philippians, 800 miles away, expressing his loving heart for them.

So the content of these verses are essential aspects of any pastor's heart for the flock he loves, and, indeed, in every Christian's life.

A Thankful Heart

In this opening section, Paul first reveals a grateful heart. He expresses to the Philippians that "I thank my God in all my remembrance of you" (**v 3**). Regardless of the difficulties of his circumstances, the believers in Philippi constantly remain at the forefront of his mind. It has been a decade since he first preached to them, but he continues to cherish this special body of believers. With every passing year, he grows increasingly grateful to God for this beloved church. Despite his present imprisonment, Paul exudes a selfless attitude, "always offering prayer" (**v 4**) for them. Though held captive in Rome, the apostle remains thankful for evidences of grace in their lives. He says that he is "offering prayer" for them. This is the language of Leviticus, as though he is a priest bringing an offering to the altar to be given to God. The intercession—praying to God on behalf of others—that Paul offers to God is his sacrifice for them. He is representing the Philippians before God, for their spiritual good. Those specific prayer requests will be detailed in verses 9-11.

Such a thankful heart in intercessory prayer for other believers demonstrated by Paul should characterize each one of us. In the midst of our own adversities, we should never lose sight of praying for others. When offering intercessory prayers, we are diverted away from our own problems to the lives of others. This kind of selfless praying is good medicine for our own troubled souls because it takes our gaze off from ourselves and refocuses it upon others.

A Joyful Spirit

A second aspect of the loving heart of Paul is revealed in his joyful spirit. He writes that he prays "with joy in my every prayer for you" (**v 4**). It is not with a self-absorbed, morbid spirit that Paul prays for them. As we read these words, we would never suspect that Paul was imprisoned. He is possessed with a triumphant joy. The tone of these words would lead us to assume that he must be attending a festival or celebrating with friends in their home. Who could imagine that he is, in fact, chained to soldiers, confined under house arrest?

Such joy is a fruit of the Spirit that only God can produce. This evidence of grace is a deep gladness in the heart that knows all is well in the Lord. Such an inner exuberance is not a feeling that is dependent upon favorable circumstances. Genuine joy runs far deeper. As we will consider when we reach Paul's teaching in Philippians 3 – 4, happiness from the world runs high when our life situations are positive. But such happiness flees when our circumstances turn unfavorable. True joy, however, is not dependent upon our earthly circumstances. Instead, it rests upon our unchanging relationship with the Lord, who is our ever-present source of joy. As the pastor and theologian John MacArthur writes:

"Spiritual joy ... is not an attitude dependent on chance or circumstances. It is a deep and abiding confidence that, regardless of one's circumstances in life, all is well between the believer and the Lord. No matter what difficulty, pain, disappointment, failure, rejection, or other challenge one is facing, genuine joy remains because of that eternal well-being established by God's grace in salvation. Thus, Scripture makes it clear that the fullest, most lasting, and satisfying joy is derived from a true relationship with God." (*The MacArthur New Testament Commentary on Philippians*, page 10)

This supernatural joy is what floods Paul's heart as he sits imprisoned in Rome. As we will be discovering, joy is a major theme that runs through this letter. "Joy" (*chara*) is used four times (**1:4**, 25; 2:2; 4:1). "Rejoice" (*chairo*) occurs eight times (1:18 [twice]; 2:17-18; 3:1; 4:4 [twice], 10). Many feel that the key verse in the book is, "Rejoice in the Lord always; again I will say, rejoice!" (4:4). Throughout this letter, a triumphant note of joy is seen in Paul's life and writing. This kind of Christianity is contagious and spreads to others, often drawing them to faith in Christ.

Does this kind of joy flood your heart? Do you know the gladness that rises above adverse circumstances? Or are there trials in your life that are presently quenching your spiritual zest? Perhaps you need to refocus upon the Lord and experience the exuberance that only he gives. Our joy runs deepest when we are on our knees before God in prayer. A good test of the depth of joy in our lives is the nature of our prayers for others.

A Gospel Focus

A third mark of Paul's loving heart toward others is seen in his unwavering gospel focus. Though chained to Roman soldiers, the apostle maintains a riveting gaze upon the saving message of Jesus Christ. Though confined under house arrest, he has not lost sight of spreading the message of salvation to others. Rather than complain about his station in life, the apostle sees this imprisonment as a new opportunity to advance the good news of Christ. This unwavering obsession with the spread of the gospel is reflected in his prayers for the Philippians. Despite his present captivity, what fills his vision and directs his emotions is his fond remembrance of their "participation in the gospel from the first day until now" (**1:5**).

This word "participation" (*koinonia*) means to share something in common with another person. Such a partnership occurs when two or more people become involved together in a joint venture. This was the case with Peter, Andrew, James, and John. These four men were partners in the same fishing business (Luke 5:3-11). They were, literally, in the same boat together. This is much like what Paul shares in common with the Philippians in the work of the gospel. Though separated by many miles, they remain in partnership together in being fishers of men and spreading the message of salvation to the world.

This joint participation in the gospel is what all believers share together. We have collectively put our trust in the same Lord and Savior, Jesus Christ. As fellow believers, it is incumbent upon us, collectively, to take this message to the world. We have been fused together by the Holy Spirit to be members of the body of Christ. Regardless of the circumstances, every Christian shares with other believers this same evangelistic enterprise, to reach the four corners of the earth with the gospel. We are in the same boat, engaged in the same profession, and we have a great deal in common with our business partners, no matter what the differences are in our languages, cultures and experiences.

> We are in the same boat, engaged in the same profession, no matter what our differences are.

A Confident Hope

Fourth, we observe Paul's loving heart in the confident hope he has for the Philippians. The apostle is convinced that they are genuinely converted to Christ. Consequently, he possesses a positive certainty about their future. He writes that he is, "confident … that He who began a good work in you will perfect it until the day of Christ Jesus" (Philippians **1:6**). This good work that God began in them commenced when the new birth made them alive in Christ. This points back to the time when Paul first preached the gospel in Philippi. God opened their hearts, and they believed the gospel. What God began, the apostle is convinced, God will complete. With a pastor's encouragement, he reassures them that they will be preserved to the end, never to fall away from grace.

Salvation is not a matter of our working for God's acceptance, but it is God working for us and in us. None of us can work our way into earning God's favor, nor can any of us through our work maintain

God's ongoing favor. God already did the work for us in the death of Christ upon the cross. Further, he graciously applied this work of Christ in us by the Spirit. Salvation is not by human achievement, but by divine accomplishment through the finished work of Jesus Christ upon the cross. This free gift was applied to our lives by the **regenerating** work of the Holy Spirit. From beginning to end, salvation is entirely a divine work of grace. If God has caused you to be born again, you can be assured that he will complete this work until "the day of Christ Jesus." As a believer in Christ, you are as certain of heaven as though you have already been there ten thousand years. God finishes what he starts.

An Affectionate Love

Fifth, Paul also expresses his deep affections for the Philippians: "I have you in my heart, since both in my imprisonment and in the defense and confirmation of the gospel, you all are partakers of grace with me" (**v 7**). Paul has strong feelings towards them because of their mutual salvation in Christ. This warm fondness is not a fleeting emotion that merely lays on the surface of his heart. To the contrary, what Paul feels for them is a deep-seated passion that has endured over the years. Like two pieces of metal welded together, his entire being is forged to them by the unbreakable bond of the Spirit.

Remarkably, Paul feels this way toward them "all." This inclusive love reveals how large-hearted he was toward the Philippians. He treasures every believer in the church as a trophy of grace. He cannot reject those whom the Lord has accepted. This genuine affection for them fills his entire being. Despite his present difficulties, Paul perseveres in his unwavering concern for them. Though being chained to Roman soldiers, Paul remains a strong witness for Christ in his "defense and confirmation of the gospel." Nothing must be allowed to compromise his testimony for Christ.

And so Paul longs for them "with the affection of Christ Jesus" (**v 8**). The word for "affection" literally means "intestines," or "internal organs." Paul is speaking **metaphorically** in order to press home the way in which he feels so deeply for them in the core of his being. This fervent affection for others must mark our lives. We must do more than simply endure other believers. We must lovingly care for them. As the twentieth-century theologian James Montgomery Boice put it:

> "It is not enough to tolerate other Christians. You must enjoy their company. You must learn from them. Furthermore, this fellowship must be one that is constantly expanding to include other Christians, even those whom you have never met but with whom you are forever united in the Lord." (*Philippians,* page 43)

No matter how **doctrinally sound** we may be, if we are without love, we are "a noisy gong or a clanging cymbal" (1 Corinthians 13:1). Without love for others, regardless of how involved we are in Christian activities, we are "nothing."

Questions for reflection

1. What happens when Christians in ministry have thin skins and tough hearts?

2. "God finishes what he starts." How does this comfort you when you face trials in life, or you are particularly aware of your own sinfulness or weakness?

3. Are you in any danger of being doctrinally sound, but without love for your church?

PART TWO

Paul's pastoral heart is revealed in his concern for the spiritual growth of the Philippians. As one who has invested much in their lives, the apostle longs that they would become more like Christ. The specifics of what he desires for them are recorded in **verses 9-11**. In what follows, we will examine the nature of the prayers he offered for this beloved church. The main thrust of his prayers for them is that they will grow in their love for one another.

These petitions should guide each one of us in our intercessions for others. This prison prayer by Paul should direct what every pastor prays for his flock. Moreover, what Paul desired for the Philippians should guide every husband and wife in praying for each other. This pastoral concern should formulate what every parent petitions God for their children. May God use these verses to direct the intensity and content of our prayers.

Love's Priority

What Paul is praying for the Philippians is that they will have a greater love for one another. He petitions God that they will grow in their love yet more and more. He begins, "And this I pray, that your love may abound still more and more" (**v 9**). The object of this love is not stated, but we can reasonably assume that he has love for other believers in view, since there are many other similar passages in which Paul opens his other letters by commending the saints for their love of the **brethren**. The priority he places upon loving other believers is repeatedly frontloaded in the opening sections of his letters (Ephesians 1:15; Colossians 1:4; 1 Thessalonians 1:3; 2 Thessalonians 1:3). So this stress that the apostle places upon Christian love for other believers is the intent here.

This love for their fellow believers will grow as a result of their deepening love for God. The more they love God, the more they will have an increased capacity to love others. Jesus affirmed this cause-

and-effect relationship. Obeying the greatest commandment, which is to love God with one's entire being, is the key to keeping the second greatest commandment, which is to love one's neighbor (Matthew 22:37-40). The former produces the latter.

This priority that Paul places upon loving other believers should occupy our prayers for others. The greatest petition we can bring before God on behalf of other Christians is that they would deepen in their love for him and for others. Paul stressed this priority elsewhere: "But now faith, hope, love, abide these three; but the greatest of these is love" (1 Corinthians 13:13). Where love of the brethren grows, the church is most like heaven and becomes attractive to the world. This same increased capacity to love others is what we must pray for our own spiritual lives.

Love's Precision

Paul prayed that the love experienced by the Philippians would be directed "in real knowledge and all discernment" (Philippians **1:9**). The Reformer John Calvin explained what Paul meant by "real knowledge," or "all knowledge":

> "[Paul] means that it is full and complete—not a knowledge of all things." (*The Epistles of Paul to the Galatians, Ephesians, Philippians and Colossians,* page 31)

Rightly exercising Christian love requires God-given insight into people and situations. It necessitates the practical wisdom that only God can impart. Genuine love never operates in a fog. Authentic love requires penetrating discernment into the real needs of people as they find themselves in real-life situations. "Real knowledge" (*epignosis*) does not refer to the mere head knowledge of facts. It means having a heart understanding of people's lives that perceives their deepest needs and how we can best meet those needs. Paul is not praying that the Philippians would become smarter, but wiser, in their care for one another. Compassion, rather than cognition, is his prayer. He requests that spiritual insight would be given to them so that they can know how best to love others.

Every Christian should be praying for other believers to possess this same heart knowledge and discernment. We cannot demonstrate love toward others until we have the spiritual wisdom to know what their real needs are. We must know how to love people before we can actually do so. Many times, we think we know what is best for other people, but we have misread the situation. Or we see it correctly, but we do not know the best way to minister to them. Certainly, we need depth of insight to assess where people are. We need discernment whenever we are counseling others. We also need spiritual perception in knowing how to encourage others. Without this God-given wisdom, our love is often misguided. But with discernment, we will be on target.

Love's Profit

As Paul prioritizes love between believers, he explains that the purpose of requesting real knowledge and discernment is "so that you may approve the things that are excellent" (**v 10**). The word "approve" (*dokimazo*) was a method used in testing metals and coins to determine whether they met specified standards. This means that Paul is praying that they will discern what is "excellent" in loving others— that is, that they will know which needs exceed all else.

> The most challenging choices are often in deciding what is good, better, and best.

As Christians, often the most difficult challenge we face is not in distinguishing between good and evil. Rather, the most challenging choices are often in deciding between what is good, better, and best in how to love others. Paul is fervently praying that his Christian brothers and sisters will know what is best—that which is "excellent"—in loving one another.

This is what we must be praying for other Christians. We must petition God on their behalf that they will discern what is "excellent" in loving others. Church members need to know how to best support one another. Every husband and wife needs to know how to best love their spouse. Only then can we pursue and practice the highest good for others. So we need to pray for this spiritual discernment in our own love for others. In reaching out to people, we need to be able to sort through the multiple options that lie before us so that we can approve and pursue those things that are "excellent."

Love's Purity

With genuine concern, Paul further prays that the Philippians will show love "in order to be sincere and blameless" (**v 10b**). True love requires a pure heart and life. The word "sincere" comes from two words for "sun" and "to judge." It was originally used to describe a piece of fine pottery that was judged in the light of the sun and found to be without any cracks. In ancient times, devious merchants would conceal flaws in their expensive pottery with wax. The authenticity of valuable pottery was revealed when held up to the light of the sun.

This word, then, indicates an authentic life of integrity. It denotes a love that is real, and which, when it comes into contact with the heat of a difficult situation or a difficult person who demands sacrifice or commitment, does not melt away. It speaks of a character that does not crack under pressure.

Paul is praying that there will be no character flaws or false love in the Philippians. Nothing must be hidden by the false cover-up of a religious façade. They must not appear to be one person on Sunday in church, but someone else on Monday in their work. There must not be an inconsistency between what they confess to believe and how they live. Every area of life must fit together into a cohesive whole. This is the idea of personal integrity or spiritual wholeness.

Moreover, Paul prays that the Philippians will prove themselves to be "blameless." This word means, literally, "not to stumble." Paul is praying that in their Christian walk the Philippians will not fall into any moral failure that causes themselves or others to stumble. Put positively, to be blameless means pursuing personal holiness in such a manner as not to give offense to others through any moral failing. The apostle asks God to make it so that in their daily walk they will not become ensnared by the world.

It matters to God how we live our lives. Forgiveness of sin does not bestow freedom to sin. The grace that pardons us is the same grace that must purify us. This kind of personal integrity should mark the daily life of every Christian. Our love for others will be demonstrated by living in such a manner as will not cause them to stumble in their Christian walk.

Love's Perseverance

In addition, Paul prays for the Philippians that their selfless love for others would be increasing "until the day of Christ" (**v 10b**). He petitions God that they would be steadfast in their love until the time of Christ's return. If Christ should **tarry**, they must persevere in their selfless love until the end. As long as they are alive, they must maintain their devotion to one another. No matter how challenging it may become in loving someone else, they must endure in doing so until the end. There is much room to press on in remaining patient, kind, and forgiving with others. *Whenever he returns,* Paul says, *let our Lord find you loving one another:*

> "The whole life must be a preparation for that great day, for it is then that the true character of every man's life will be revealed, and everyone will be judged according to his work."
>
> (Hendriksen, *Philippians,* page 61)

This prayer of Paul should challenge us to be praying along the same lines for other believers. No matter what wrong those for whom we pray have suffered and no matter what trials they are walking through, they must maintain their genuine concern for others. Regardless of how they have been disappointed and hurt, they must endure in loving others without wavering. Those for whom we pray need us to pray that they would remain faithful in their pursuit of loving God and loving others until the day of Christ Jesus. And, of course, we are in no less need of praying this for ourselves than others are of our prayers for them.

How Love is Produced

Paul indicates more of what he is praying for the Philippians when he recognizes that they have "been filled with the fruit of righteousness which comes through Jesus Christ" (**v 11**). This "fruit of righteousness" first began to sprout and grow in their lives at the time of their conversion. This is a practical righteousness that produces personal conformity to the person of Jesus Christ. This supernatural fruit was not self-generated by the Philippians. It can only come "through Jesus Christ." This spiritual fruit is the life of Christ lived out in believers. The first evidence of this "fruit of the Spirit" is love, meaning love for others (Galatians 5:22).

This practical righteousness was first produced at conversion. Putting our faith in Christ is the cause, and loving others is the effect. Rebirth is the root, and love is the fruit. Put another way, the new heart given in the new birth leads to love for other believers. This fruit of practical righteousness will be clearly evidenced in the lives of true believers.

The Pinnacle of Love

Throughout this prayer, we have been glimpsing Paul's heart. And he concludes this opening section by expressing his highest desire for their spiritual lives. He prays that love for others would abound "to the glory and praise of God" (Philippians **1:11**). As the Philippians grow in their love for one another, this kind of life rises to the highest level. This results in giving honor to God. This is the *summum bonum* of Christian living—the highest good in life. The ultimate goal in Paul's prayers for them is for the praise and glory of God. This chief end must be the supreme motivation for everything they do. Paul wrote to the church in Corinth, "Whether, then, you eat or drink or whatever you do, do all to the glory of God" (1 Corinthians 10:31). Such an all-inclusive statement means that all activity must be directed by this one master passion. A church's growing love for others will bring great praise to God.

This overarching theme of living for the glory of God should be our supreme goal. The **Puritan** Thomas Brooks wrote:

"The aim of the obedient soul, in prayer and praises, in talking and walking, in giving and receiving, in living and doing, is divine glory."

(*Heaven on Earth: A Treatise on Christian Assurance*, page 234)

God alone is worthy of all praise. He will not share his glory with another, and we should never suggest by how we live and love that he ought to. In all that we do, the pursuit and promotion of the glory of God must be our all-consuming passion.

Paul's Prayers and Yours

This prayer by Paul for the Philippians provides a helpful, concise checklist that can and should direct our prayers for others. What he prayed for these believers should guide our prayers for one another. As an unconditional love grows in us for other believers, we will be praying for them. The fruit of righteousness that began to be evident at our conversion will grow as we offer prayers on behalf of others. May God enable us to approve the things that are excellent until the day of Christ. Should he return in your lifetime, may he find you using that life to love his people. And in so doing, may you, and those for whom you pray, bring great glory and praise of God.

Questions for reflection

1. How has this chapter caused you to want to pray?

2. How has it helped you know what you will pray?

3. We "must not appear to be one person on Sunday in church, but someone else on Monday in [our] work." When do you find yourself living inauthentically? How could you see these times opportunities to love and serve your Lord?

3. THE INDOMITABLE SERVANT

A man on a mission, Paul traveled extensively to the major cities of the Roman Empire in order to preach the gospel. He purposefully targeted the heavily populated centers of Macedonia and Greece such as Philippi, Thessalonica, Corinth, Athens, and more. To reach these cities with the message of Jesus Christ was to send an influence to their surrounding regions.

But most of all, Paul wanted to preach Christ in Rome, because Rome was the most important city of the empire. The Imperial City boasted a population of over one million people and showcased its magnificent buildings, including the Emperor's Palace, the Forum, and the Circus Maximus. Rome was the nerve center of power for this ancient superpower. To penetrate Rome with the gospel would be to send out a ripple effect across the Empire and the known world.

Not How He Had Planned

At last, Paul did fulfill his desire to travel to Rome in order to preach the unsearchable riches of Christ. But he did not go there under the circumstances he had anticipated—as an open-air evangelist preaching in the amphitheaters and public arenas. Instead, he went to Rome as a prisoner in chains. He was arrested in Jerusalem and sent to Rome in order to stand trial before Caesar, where he would probably have his life taken by the death penalty. Upon his arrival, he was imprisoned under house arrest for two long years from AD 60 to 61. Rather than being free to preach to the masses, Paul was confined to one small house as he awaited his trial from Caesar and the final verdict that would follow.

Despite these difficult circumstances, Paul nevertheless preached some of the greatest sermons that ever came from his lips while here in Rome. However, these messages were not delivered to large, swelling crowds, but to the emperor's guards, one-on-one. In turn, the truth was eventually received by the guards, who carried it into the palace of Caesar. These new believers carried the gospel where Paul could never have gone, into the very household of Caesar himself. Those around the emperor were being converted by the witness that Paul had given to the **praetorian guard**. These soldiers were the most elite Roman guards in the entire empire. They were the personal bodyguards for Caesar, and served in his imperial palace. They were often the powers of influence near the throne and exerted a persuasion upon the emperor's understanding and decisions. The apostle preached every sermon while in chains to these men who were being rotated through his rented house. From there, the gospel advanced into the very headquarters of the empire and beyond.

So in this passage, Paul updates the Philippians on his situation in his Roman imprisonment, and though under house arrest, he is rejoicing triumphantly in Christ. The Philippians have heard the troubling reports of the difficulties that have overtaken their beloved former pastor. They have learned that he has been arrested, sent to Rome, suffered shipwreck, and has been imprisoned. They are deeply concerned for their former spiritual shepherd. Is Paul still in chains? Has he come to trial yet? Has a verdict been given? Is he still alive?

In order to answer these questions, Paul writes to give them this update concerning his condition. He affirms that many of the reports they have heard are true. He is, in fact, still in chains, and his future remains uncertain. Yet, he wants them to know that all these difficulties have worked out for the greater furtherance of the gospel of Jesus Christ—and for the first and greatest missionary of the church that alone is sufficient cause to rejoice.

Confidence Instead of Complaint

Despite his imprisonment, Paul remained confident in the spread of the gospel of Jesus Christ. "Now I want you to know, brethren, that my circumstances have turned out for the greater progress of the gospel" (Philippians **1:12**). He acknowledges his imprisonment, which from a human perspective is dire. Here is the mighty apostle, captured and contained like a chained animal. Yet from the divine perspective, this unexpected impediment has turned out for the greater spread of the gospel. Paul's concern is not for his own personal safety but for the truth of Jesus Christ to move forward, whatever it costs him. The word "progress" (*prokope*) means "to move out." Just as a pioneer advances into uncharted territory so that others may come in behind, so also Paul sees his confinement as a catalyst for the gospel to launch forward.

As Paul discusses his imprisonment, he does not want personal sympathy from the Philippians. He is not complaining in order to manipulate people to feel sorry for him. Neither does he have a martyr spirit. His aim is that his readers will be more confident in their own witness for the gospel. He updates them concerning this difficulty so that, in the face of the opposition to the gospel, they too will stand up and testify for the Lord Jesus Christ. This news is designed to embolden them.

This report by Paul should have the same effect upon us as well. In the face of whatever resistance we face for the gospel, whether at work or home or with friends, we, too, must speak the truth with increasing confidence. We must be persuaded that whatever obstacles we face in our witnessing, they are not impediments to the message of Jesus Christ. Rather, what we view as obstacles are often opportunities to further the advance of this saving message. The great nineteenth-century theologian B.B. Warfield put this wonderfully well:

> "In the infinite wisdom of the Lord of all the earth, each event falls with exact precision into its proper place in this unfolding of his eternal plan." (*Biblical Doctrines,* page 22)

We must be convinced that God can use every instance of opposition to advance the cause of his kingdom in the proclamation of the gospel of Jesus Christ. What difficulties are you facing? Do you see how they can be used by Christ?

The Calling of the Chains

Paul now gives some specific details about his present confinement: "my imprisonment in the cause of Christ has become well known throughout the whole praetorian guard and to everyone else" (**v 13**). The word "imprisonment" comes from a root word (*desmon*) that means "bonds that are made with chains." Paul elsewhere identifies himself as "an ambassador in chains" (Ephesians 6:20; see also Acts 28:20). For two years, Paul was fastened in chains that were probably extended handcuffs about 18 inches long. These chains were always attached to his wrist and restricted his every movement. The praetorian guard were rotated through his rented quarters, and his chains were never removed. Day and night, Paul was only 18 inches away from a Roman soldier. In this changing of the guards, there were probably several dozen soldiers who were circulating through his room and were attached to him at various times.

Despite this confinement, Paul does not see himself as a prisoner of Rome. Instead, he identifies himself as "a prisoner of the Lord" (Ephesians 4:1), believing he is there by divine appointment. His imprisonment is "in the cause of Christ" (Philippians **1:13**); and this imprisonment and that cause "has become well known," because the news has spread far and wide. Even the Philippians, as far as 600 miles away, have heard about it. And so, as Boice wrote,

> "Paul's suffering was neither corrective nor instructive. It was simply a suffering permitted by God so that the gospel might be spread to others." (*Philippians,* page 52)

In Rome, Paul's confinement in chains is well known "throughout the whole praetorian guard." These high-level soldiers who have become a captive audience to Paul—he is chained to them, but they are also chained to him! Paul could not escape from them; but they could not escape from his witness for Christ. He had a new congregation with every new shift.

Every one of us should learn and take heart from this. No matter what hard place in which we may find ourselves, God can use us to advance his word in that very situation. Where is it that you feel restricted in life? Could it be in a difficult job? Maybe you are tied to your desk. Maybe you feel confined to your house with little children. Maybe you are a salesman and confined to your car. Maybe you are a schoolteacher and feel trapped in a secular classroom. Maybe you are a high-school student and tied to your class schedule. Wherever you find yourself, you can see your adverse situation as an opportunity to give testimony for Christ where one would not otherwise exist.

You are not where you are by accident. You are where you are by divine appointment, for the purposes of sharing the gospel.

One Believer on Fire

And, Paul explains, as a result of his imprisonment, the believers in Rome have far more boldness and courage to tell others about Christ. "Most of the brethren, trusting in the Lord because of my imprisonment, have far more courage to speak the word of God without fear" (**v 14**). Paul's outspokenness while in chains has highly motivated his fellow believers to do the same for Christ. Paul reports that they are "without fear" in giving their witness for the gospel. No longer are they hesitant to mention the name of Christ, as presumably they have been previously. They are now without fear of rejection or reprisals in speaking for the Savior. They see that Paul is willing to suffer for the gospel, and able to rejoice even when he has lost both liberty and security—and this example and challenge exerts an enormous effect upon them.

Paul explains that the believers in Rome are bearing witness for Christ by "trusting in the Lord." They are *challenged* by Paul's example—but their *trust* does not rest in him. Instead, they are putting their trust in *Christ* and they are doing this, as he writes, "because of my imprisonment." Without Paul being in chains, the church in Rome would be much weaker in their evangelistic enterprise. Without his imprisonment, Caesar's household would remain a hellhole. Apart from his incarceration, the citizens of Rome would not be openly talking about the gospel. But because of Paul's chains, the praetorian guard are being won to faith in Jesus Christ, and the word is spreading like wildfire throughout Caesar's own household. In fact, the saints in Caesar's household are greeting the saints in Philippi (4:22). Further, the people on the street are witnessing for the Lord. Because of Paul's imprisonment, the church in Rome has been filled with a new boldness to speak the word of God without the fear of man.

> One believer on fire for God can embolden thousands with new courage.

We learn from this that one believer on fire for God can embolden thousands with new courage to bear witness for Christ. As we have seen, this is what happened with Paul in Rome. It also happened with Martin Luther in sixteenth-century Germany and with John Knox in sixteenth-century Scotland. It happened with George Whitefield in the American colonies and Susannah Wesley in England in the 1700s. It occurred with Charles Spurgeon in Victorian London. One man or woman lit up for God has the capacity to put steel into the backbone of countless believers who live, work and witness around them. This is the influence of one person when he or she speaks the word of God with courage.

Think about how God can use you to influence other believers for Christ in this same way. As you speak up for him, others are encouraged to do the same. Your example will be contagious, affecting both believers and unbelievers. Will you emulate Paul's example and be an open witness for Christ? Will your circumstances cause you to shrink from preaching the gospel, or will they be used by you to

magnify the gospel? What might be the effect if you live on fire for
Christ as Paul did?

Questions for reflection

1. List out the difficulties you are facing right now in life. How might
    they be used by Christ to further his kingdom work?

2. Who do you know who, like Paul, is willing to suffer for the gos-
    pel and rejoice in adversity? How will you let them be an example
    and challenge to you?

3. "One believer on fire for God can embolden thousands ... to bear
    witness for Christ." Would you pray for such Spirit-given fire for
    yourself?

PART TWO

The Pastor and His Critics

Every great preacher has had his critics within the church. John Calvin was exiled from his pulpit in Geneva, Switzerland after only two years. Jonathan Edwards was voted out of his pastorate after over twenty-two years as the pastor in Northampton, Connecticut—and that by a ninety-percent vote. Charles Spurgeon suffered severe discouragement, if not depression, from the leaders in his own denomination during the **Downgrade Controversy**. No pastor who preaches the truth is without his critics.

It was no different for the apostle. Remarkably, other ministers in the capital city had become jealous of Paul. "Some, to be sure, are preaching Christ even from envy and strife" (**1:15**). By Paul's own admission, these preachers in Rome were genuinely proclaiming Christ. They were not false teachers, but those who were rightly preaching Christ and him crucified. The problem was not with their message, but with their motives. They were heralding Christ, but they were driven by envy. The word *phthonos* means a jealousy of or a feeling of ill will toward others. In this case, their rotten attitude was toward Paul. They were attacking his reputation by casting doubt on his character. Perhaps they were insinuating that Paul was in prison because of God's **chastisement** upon his life: that if Paul were truly walking with the Lord, he would not be in prison.

Maybe they were envious of Paul's apostolic authority. Maybe they were jealous of his towering intellect or gifted speech. It could be that they coveted his far-reaching influence. Whatever it was, they considered Paul to be a threat to their following in their ministries. The result of this envy was "strife" (*eris*), meaning a heated contention, mean quarreling, wrangling of words, unhealthy debate, and harmful arguing. This strife could be devastating to the spiritual health of the churches in Rome. It would create divisions in the churches among believers, forcing people to make a choice between supporting Paul or standing with these petty preachers. Sadly, many believers in Rome, influenced by Paul's opponents, were turning their backs on the most influential follower of Christ who ever lived: the apostle Paul.

What causes such envy? It is produced by learning about the advantage of someone else instead of you. It might be that a colleague becomes successful at work and is promoted instead of you. It could be that another person is asked to teach or sing at church instead of you. Whatever the specifics, someone else is being recognized and praised instead of you. Rather than being content with where you are and what you have, seeds of jealousy are sown into your heart.

Still Standing Together

Despite these opponents, some preachers in Rome rightfully stood with Paul: "some also [preach Christ] from good will" (**v 15**). These other preachers did not spread the anti-Paul propaganda, but preached Christ with entirely different motives. They ministered with "good will," which means "pure motives." Paul says that "the latter do it out of love, knowing that I am appointed for the defense of the gospel" (**v 16**). This second group preached Christ out of a pure love for Jesus Christ and a passion for his gospel.

Love for God and envy of others cannot co-exist in the same heart at the same time. When envy moves in, love moves out. These spiritually-minded preachers were deeply concerned for the apostle Paul, who was now suffering imprisonment. This was a time to stand with the man of God, not to slander him. They were motivated by loyalty, not by envy.

Why? Because these godly preachers believed that Paul was appointed for the defense of the gospel. They acknowledged that it was God who sovereignly commissioned him to preach it and protect it against all attacks. They understood that Paul was in prison because of his boldness in the gospel. Even in his suffering, they saw that he remained true to the message of saving grace. This is the high price of preaching of the gospel.

You and I need such fellow believers who will stand with us in our attempts to make Christ known. We need people who will not be swayed by the divisive gossip of others but who will faithfully bear witness for Christ. Their loyalty bolsters our commitment to persevere through tough times. Do you have people like this near you? And are you this type of person to those near you who are walking through trials?

Motives Matter

Paul returns to address the first group of envious preachers. He writes, "the former proclaim Christ out of selfish ambition rather than from pure motives, thinking to cause me distress in my imprisonment" (**v 17**). "Selfish ambition" literally means "one working for hire." It was used of someone who could be bought with money in order to carry out a devious deed. These Christians are evidently in it for what they can personally get out of it, and not for what they can sacrificially give to others. Though they exalt Christ in their words, they use their ministry to promote themselves. They lift Christ up only in order to lift themselves up.

> It matters not only what we say and do, but why we do it.

These preachers are vicious in their attacks on Paul, "thinking to cause me distress in my imprisonment" (**v 17**). This "distress" is an attempt to shame Paul by shaping public opinion against Paul. They slander his character and discredit his motives in order to gain back their own following. This "distress" refers to the emotional anguish that they are intending to cause Paul. They intend to degrade him by inflicting shame upon his reputation.

The motives of every believer in ministry are critically important to God. It matters not only what we say and do, but why we do it. We can conceal selfish motives while serving Christ. We must never use our ministry for Christ as a cover-up to hide our own self-promoting agenda. The purest motives require that we do all things for the glory of God.

Every one of us faces assaults by others who would steal our joy. As Christians, we are not immune from such difficulties in life. It may be a co-worker in ministry who threatens our joy. It may be someone in your small-group Bible study. Or another person in the choir where you sing. It could be a fellow student in a Christian school. Or another minister in your city. There are individuals who are brought into our lives who threaten our joy. This is why we must remain riveted in our focus upon Christ.

In This I Rejoice

What is Paul's response to this conflict? It is utterly remarkable. The apostle tells us that he has constant joy. "What then? Only that in every way, whether in pretense or in truth, Christ is proclaimed; and in this I rejoice. Yes, and I will rejoice" (**v 18**). Paul answers his own question by asserting that what really matters is not that he is exonerated, but that the name of Christ is exalted. What a dynamic witness this humble servant of Christ was giving to the Philippians! Even when thrown into prison, when others are turning against him, and when his good name was being slandered, Paul was rejoicing in the Lord.

These envious preachers are carrying out their ministry in "pretense" (*prophasis*) (**v 18**)—they are characterized by hypocrisy. A "hypocrisy" involved putting on a mask. An actor would be given a script and assume a character part. He stepped onto a stage and played an assigned role, often wearing either a smiling or a frowning mask. He would pretend to be someone he was not. When the play was over, he would step off the stage, take off the mask, and return to being who he really was. And these ministers are doing exactly the same: putting on a religious mask and acting pious. But the appearance that they are close to God is all a mask, while they sway and manipulate people. With penetrating insight, Paul sees it for what it is. He rips off their masks and exposes their rotten pretense and foul deception.

Paul refers to the second group of preachers in the opposite manner. They preach "in truth." There is no hypocrisy here, but only genuine pure motives that exalt Christ. These humble servants preach Christ out of love for their Lord and his people, including his apostle, knowing that Paul was appointed for the defense of the gospel. They are truthful before others as they carry out their ministry. There is no mask in their lives, but only transparency before God.

Throughout this painful ordeal, Paul continues to concentrate upon Christ. This is the third time in these few verses that Paul speaks of Christ being proclaimed. The priority for Paul is always the magnification of his Master. He is not preoccupied with escaping his suffering, nor with rebutting his foes. Paul has a much higher agenda. He is concerned about the name of Christ going forward. For Paul, it matters little what happens to him or what is said about him—as long as the Lord Jesus is glorified. The advancement of the gospel is everything to the apostle. In spite of his fiery trial, Paul can rejoice because Christ is being preached. John MacArthur shows how this can be our reaction too:

"Paul's example of selfless humility shows that the worse circumstances are the greater the joy can be. When the seemingly secure things in life begin to collapse, when suffering and sorrow increase, believers should be drawn into ever-deeper fellowship with the Lord." (*The MacArthur New Testament Commentary on Philippians,* page 69)

Do you rejoice in the midst of your suffering when you see the name of Christ being advanced? Do you care more about your reputation or your **Redeemer**'s? It is a challenge for every one of us to maintain this perspective. God has placed us in different circumstances, with different trials being brought to bear upon us. Whatever may be confronting us, we must rejoice in the Lord as we see our adversity as advancing the gospel. We are prevented from collapsing in our affliction as we recognize that Christ is being made known. We must recognize that our life is not about us being comfortable, but about Christ being made known.

The Pillow of God's Sovereignty

How could Paul's joy be so resilient? How could his priority be his Lord? The answer lies in the fact that he had a deep certainty in the Lord's sovereign purposes for his life: "I know that this will turn out for my deliverance" (**v 19**). This word "know" means to know something is certain. Paul's joy is deeply grounded in his convictions about God himself. Paul knows he will soon be released from this imprisonment one way or another, either by death or by dismissal. Paul believes that his life is held in the hands of the sovereign God. It is this conviction in the overruling authority of God that gives him great joy. He would be filled with fear if he did not trust in this formidable truth. He would have no joy if he thought that his circumstances were governed by mere random chance. Paul lays his head on the pillow of the sovereignty of God each night—and he sleeps well on it.

It is the Holy Spirit who provides the power and peace that Paul needs to remain steadfast in this difficult time (**v 19**), so that he can live with "earnest expectation and hope" (**v 20**). "Earnest expectation" means literally "to stretch the neck forward." The idea is one of straining to look ahead to the future. "Hope" refers to the certain confidence that God will cause all things to work together for his glory and his good (Romans 8:28). Paul stretches forward in his mind and is confident in the hope of the future. Consequently, Paul believes that God will use even these petty preachers in Rome for the greater furtherance of the gospel. God has this situation squarely in the palm of his hand and fully under his control.

> Paul lays his head on the pillow of the sovereignty of God—and he sleeps well on it.

And so even amid these difficulties, Paul has the resounding confidence that he "will not be put to shame in anything" (Philippians **1:20**).

He knows he will stand trial before Caesar and be examined about his faith in Christ. By God's grace, he will be made strong and confident in that hour. It is notable how often Paul asks his believing friends to pray for his witness: "Pray on my behalf, that utterance may be given to me in the opening of my mouth, to make known with boldness the mystery of the gospel" (Ephesians 6:19). "[Pray for us] that God will open up to us a door for the word; so that we may speak forth the mystery of Christ, for which I have also been imprisoned" (Colossians 4:3). He is in prison because he preached Christ, and repeatedly asks for prayer not for release or relief, but for courage to continue to testify to Christ.

After all, what Paul most longs for is that "Christ will even now, as always, be exalted in my body" (Philippians **1:20**). Everything is about the magnification of Christ. Every trial is seen through the lens of advancing the name of Christ. Life and death are both opportunities to serve that great end. What a perspective! Remember, Paul does not know what will be the outcome of his pending trial. He does not know at this point that he will be released from this imprisonment and preach for another six years. All he presently knows is that he is staring death in the face and does not know what the future will be. But he knows and trusts the One who does know all things, who is with him by his Spirit in life and who will, whenever and however it comes, bring him through death.

Simply put, our greatest joy in life is to know Jesus Christ. Such gladness of heart comes from far more than merely knowing about Christ. This kind of triumphant bliss is found in actually knowing him personally, in intimate relationship. Our greatest excitement is having Christ live in us and, in turn, our living for him. Those who know Christ have an unlimited supply of joy available to them in the all-sufficient person of Christ—wherever they find themselves, and whatever anyone says.

Questions for reflection

1. "When envy moves in, love moves out." Have you experienced this in your own life? What were the consequences for yourself and others around you?

2. Why is it liberating to live caring more about our Redeemer than our own reputation?

3. What will it look like for you to lay your head on the "pillow" of the sovereignty of God each night?

4. READY TO DIE, ABLE TO LIVE

No one is ready to live until they are ready to die.

You must know that the end of your life is certain before you will joyfully risk danger day by day. The end of your life must be secure before the present can be stable. It is only when you know that death will usher you into the presence of God that you will live with fearless faith.

This is precisely where the apostle Paul finds himself. He is a man staring death square in the eyes. Yet he is living with an unwavering mission for the gospel. As the apostle awaits his trial, the news of his imprisonment in Rome has reached the church in Philippi. His former flock is deeply concerned for the welfare of this man who is their spiritual father. In response, the believers in Philippi have taken up a collection to pay for the rent he must pay for his house arrest. He is the one who first brought the gospel to them, and so this church is deeply troubled for their previous pastor who is now in chains. They are concerned whether Paul will survive this imprisonment.

Paul wants his friends to know that, if need be, he is ready to die for his faith in Jesus Christ. In fact, he affirms that even if his life is taken, this loss will result in greater gain because his execution will usher him into the immediate presence of Jesus Christ. The Philippians have sought to encourage Paul and now he, in turn, writes to encourage them. He now comforts them with his bold courage in the face of death.

All believers who know for certain that Jesus Christ is Lord and Savior share this same certain future. For those in Christ, death becomes the means of graduating to glory and gaining access into the presence of Christ. Such a sure hope gives us confidence to live day by day to the fullest. This certainty regarding death is liberating as we live our daily lives.

To Live Is...

Paul begins this section by making one of the most dramatic statements to come from his pen, or anyone else's throughout history. This strong pronouncement reveals the heartbeat that should be pulsating in every Christian: "For to me, to live is Christ and to die is gain" (**v 21**). Whether anyone else lives for Christ, Paul asserts, he will. In other words, Paul says, *Regardless of what my friends or foes are doing, I will live for Christ.* To live for Christ is not referring to a mere existence; not everyone alive actually lives. Rather, he means to live life as God intended him to live, namely, for Christ. He is resolved to live with this single purpose for Christ.

The word "is" is supplied by the translator for readability, but is not found in the original language. Paul literally wrote this: "For to me to live Christ." The omission of "is" makes this statement dramatically emphatic. As the apostle is waiting his trial and possible death, he is unwavering in his single-minded devotion to Christ. With his day in court before him, the outcome is unknown to him. His life is presently flashing before his eyes. In such a sobering situation, Paul makes this bold confession of faith. His whole life is consumed with Christ. Everything in his life is bound up in Christ. The passionate pursuit of his whole being is to know and glorify Christ. The sum and substance of his present state is confined in Christ. Every moment of every day is lived for Christ.

This is what it means to be a Christian. It involves living primarily and pre-eminently for Christ. Everything else in life is secondary. The late British minister John Stott put it like this:

"Take Christ from Christianity, and you disembowel it; there is practically nothing left. Christ is the centre of Christianity, all else is circumference." (*Basic Christianity*, page 27)

The term "Christian" was first used in Acts 11:26 and means "a little Christ." It was originally a slur, coined by the world to ridicule and mock the early disciples in Antioch. The unbelievers identified them in this slanderous way, associating them with Jesus Christ, whom they saw as a common criminal crucified upon a Roman cross. But the early church embraced this title as a badge of honor. They loved being identified with Christ, even by this derisive name.

From this same prison cell, Paul would similarly write that Christ "is our life" (Colossians 3:4). That is to say, a Christian's entire life is found in Christ. Earlier, he had written, "It is no longer I who live, but Christ lives in me; and the life which I now live in the flesh I live by faith in the Son of God, who loved me and gave himself up for me" (Galatians 2:20). In other words, Paul's entire life was Christ living in him. When Paul was laid hold of by Christ, he forsook everything so that he might have the one "in whom are hidden all the treasures of wisdom and understanding" (Colossians 2:3). Nothing else compares to the surpassing value of knowing Christ.

Is this the same single focus of your life? For you to live, is it Jesus Christ? Have you found Christ to be everything in your life? Can you say that to live is Christ? This is what it means to be a genuine Christian. It means to live in Christ and for Christ.

Death Is Gain

Paul then adds, "To die is gain" (Philippians **1:21**). Again, the word "is" is supplied by the translators. Again, the verb was intentionally left off by Paul in order to make a stronger impression upon his readers. This omission gives a powerful punch to what he is saying. For him, to die is a far greater gain than living.

"Gain" means to receive a great profit. Paul realizes that death will usher him to a much greater gain. The grave will graduate him to glory. Death will deliver him into the immediate presence of Jesus Christ. Death means inestimable gain because it will usher him before the throne of Jesus Christ. Death will not be a tragedy, but a triumph. Here is the secret to living confidently as believers. The Puritan Richard Sibbes wrote:

> "What greater encouragement can a man have to fight against his enemy than when he is sure of the victory before he fights?"
>
> (*The Works of Richard Sibbes*, Volume IV, page 223)

What is most important in heaven is not the streets of gold, nor the gates of pearl. The greatest gain of being in heaven is not even to be reunited with loved ones. The greatest profit will be to stand before Christ and behold him as he is. The glory of heaven is found in Jesus Christ himself. Death will bring Paul to the Lord Jesus Christ. What greater gain can there be than this?

The best day of this life will be the last one.

As Christians, you and I must see death in this light. The world does not because it cannot. It must deny death and seek to ignore it, or despair over death and be crushed by the reality of it. We can live with the liberating knowledge that the best day of this life will be the last one. The grave is not sovereign, but only a servant to bring us to Christ. Do you have this confidence? Do you believe that to die is gain? If you live for Christ, then to die will be gain. However, if we live for anyone or anything else other than Christ, death will be loss.

Paul's Dilemma

Living for Christ creates an intense struggle within Paul. Here is his dilemma: "But if I am to live on in the flesh, this will mean fruitful labor for me; and I do not know which to choose" (**v 22**). As he prepares to stand trial, he acknowledges that the imperial verdict might spare his life. And he is so excited about seeing his Lord face to face that this would almost be a disappointment!

Still, if he is acquitted and released, he will resume his itinerant ministry for Christ. This regained freedom will give him an extended opportunity to preach the gospel in many places to countless people. This will result in more people hearing the message of Christ, and more will be saved. Further, more churches will be planted, more believers will be matured, and more young men like Timothy will be trained to preach the word. If Paul's life is spared, there will be more spiritual fruit produced that will glorify God.

In light of this dilemma, Paul admits, "I do not know which to choose." Such indecisiveness is unlike Paul. The apostle was a resolute man who was most decisive. Yet here he finds himself inwardly paralyzed, not knowing which way to choose. However, the choice is not really for Paul to make. In one sense, the outcome rests in the hands of Caesar. But in another sense, this matter is in the hands of the Lord, who sovereignly controls the emperor's decision. Solomon, a king himself, understood this: "The king's heart is like channels of water in the hand of the LORD; He turns it wherever He wishes" (Proverbs 21:1). Nevertheless, Paul is wrestling with this quandary. Death will take him to be with Christ, but an acquittal will release him to preach Christ.

We face this same dilemma whenever we see a believing loved one face death. This is true when a believing parent or friend comes to the time of their departure from this world. We are often pulled in these two opposite directions. We want God to extend their life to remain with us. Yet their condition deteriorates to the place where it is better for them to pass into heaven. At such times, we are pulled in both directions. However, we know that because of the certain future of every believer, it is better for them to leave this world to be with Christ. Such a future is much better. To die is gain.

Questions for reflection

1. What did you make of the statement, "No one is ready to live until they are ready to die"?

2. What is your own view of death? Are there any ways in which you are influenced by your culture's perspective on it, rather than a Christian one?

3. Do you feel the dilemma Paul did, either on your own behalf or that of a believing loved one? How is it comforting to live in this way?

PART TWO

Caught Between Death and Life

To live is Christ and to die is gain. This is Paul's settled outlook on his present and his future, and he further reveals his heart when he writes, "But I am hard-pressed from both directions, having the desire to depart and be with Christ, for that is very much better" (Philippians **1:23**). By this imagery, the apostle pictures himself as though walking on a narrow road with two tight walls pressing in on both sides. The walls are squeezing in tighter and tighter. This veteran missionary is "hard-pressed" from both sides. Death is closing in on one side, with ongoing life on the other. He is caught in between. He feels like he is being crushed from both sides at once. It is as though he is trapped in a vice grip. One part of him wants to be with the Lord. Another part of him realizes the need to continue serving here.

And the former fuels the latter. The commentator Gordon Fee writes:

"Even though [Paul] throws himself with abandon into life in the present, the entire orientation of his life is toward the (absolutely certain) future." (*Paul's Letter to the Philippians,* page 145)

When Paul states his "desire to depart and be with Christ" (**v 23**), "desire" (*epithumia*) indicates a strong affection or intense longing. This is not a mere passing whim. Rather, it represents a burning passion that is ignited within his heart. It is a growing zeal within him to be with Christ. "Depart" (*analuo*) is an intense word that means to loosen something. It pictures a ship tied to the dock with a rope, and a sailor loosens it, releasing the ship from the dock. This is how Paul sees his life. The rope of his life is being loosened by the approach of death. Once firmly tied to this world, he sees his life is now being loosened, releasing him to heaven.

"Depart" was also used of soldiers who were ready to break camp in order to move out to the next destination. One would loosen the ropes of the tent in preparation for continuing their journey. Paul realizes that his stakes are being pulled up, and he is being loosened from this world. He has not yet departed, but he can feel his ropes being untied. His departure will take him to his next destination. In glory, he will be in intimate association with the Lord. Paul knew that death would mean a blessed departure.

Paul reasons that death will be "very much better" (**v 23**). How can this be? Being with Christ is better than living in this sinful world. In fact, it is more than merely better or even much better. He says it is very much better. These three words—"very much better"—express the superlative degree. As his life is being loosened from this world, he is ready to sail out of this life into a far greater port in glory. Such a departure will be far better than sitting in his prison cell in chains (and, indeed, than sitting in a palace throne room in finery). Paul's heart is throbbing for heaven and to be in the presence of Christ.

This desire to be in heaven is a healthy longing for every Christian. We are strangers and aliens in this world (1 Peter 2:11). This planet is not our home. Christ has been preparing a dwelling place for us in heaven (John 14:2-3). There should be an ever growing desire within us to be in the immediate presence of Christ. There we will see him face to face. We will behold him, but not as he once was, as the humble carpenter or meek Messiah. Instead, we will gaze upon him as the glorified King and sovereign Lord over all the universe. To die is gain.

The Reason to Remain

Though Paul wrestles with this dilemma, he concludes that to remain is better for the church: "To remain on in the flesh is more necessary for your sake" (Philippians **1:24**). In his mind, he is being pulled in both directions like a rope in a tug-of-war. He wants to live on the one hand, but desires to be with the Lord on the other hand. Despite his greater desire to depart to be with Christ, he concedes that he is willing to remain here as a lesser option. Why? For the sake of the Philippians and others like them. He will deny himself his greater desire for the spiritual good of the church.

This is the debate that is raging within the apostle Paul as he writes. It is the internal conflict between what is "very much better" (**v 23**) and what is "more necessary" (**v 24**). Paul is pulled back and forth between the superiority of being with Christ, and the necessity of living for the spiritual good of others. With the apostle, what is "more necessary" for others trumps what is "very much better" for himself.

Here is the internal battle that every Christian faces. It is the struggle between what I want to do and what is best for others. We face this dilemma every day, though it is not always in life-and-death decisions. Will I do what I want to do, or will I do what is best for others? We face it at home with our families. We are confronted with it at church in ministry. What dilemma like this you might be facing? What back-and-forth struggle are you wrestling with between self-desires and self-dying? What is more necessary for your family? What is the greater good for your spouse and children? What is the highest good for your ministry and the spread of the gospel? We must be willing to sacrifice our personal desires for the greater benefit of others.

So Paul finally comes to a decision in this internal struggle. He arrives at a place where he is willing to postpone his desired departure to be with Christ. He does so for the greater needs of the church: "Convinced of this, I know that I will remain and continue with you all for your progress and joy in the faith" (**v 25**). "Convinced" (*peitho*) means that Paul is firmly persuaded. This word carries the idea of being convinced by strong argument. He knows that it is more necessary for him to stay and serve the churches. This is an act of self-denial on his part as he puts the needs of other believers before his own desires.

When Paul writes, "I know," he is convinced that his thinking about this decision is sound. He knows that he needs to remain on the earth in order to serve the churches. If God chooses, he will stay so that he may continue to preach the word and build up the believers. He is willing to delay his desired departure in order to remain here for the spiritual good of the believers in Philippi and elsewhere.

Paul explains that his release from imprisonment will be "for your progress" (**v 25**). The extension of Paul's life will be for their progress in spiritual growth. Paul's conviction is that if he lives, it is **providentially** for their growth in the grace and knowledge of the Lord Jesus Christ. Paul's life exemplifies a servant's attitude, which is committed to ministering to others. Even the most mature believers in Philippi still need Paul to help them develop into greater spiritual maturity. Paul knows that his release from prison would be for their "joy." This joy would be the result of their spiritual growth into greater Christ-likeness. All genuine joy is the result of growing closer to the Lord Jesus. As the Philippians develop in their sanctification, they will grow deeper in authentic joy. Paul adds that this joy is "in the faith," referring to the Christian faith. True joy is found in knowing and living out the body of truth recorded in Scripture. "The faith" refers to "the apostles' teaching" (Acts 2:42) and "sound **doctrine**" (Titus 2:1), as in "the faith which was once for all handed down to the saints" (Jude 3).

> Your spiritual life is strongest when your desire for the Scriptures is greatest.

Growth in the Christian life necessitates the internalization of the word of God. Growth in the Scripture and in sanctification are inseparably bound together. Jesus prayed, "Sanctify them in the truth; Your word is truth" (John 17:17). The truth of the word is the instrument used by God to bring out Christ-likeness. A steady diet of the word is essential to every believer's spiritual health. Paul urges elsewhere, "Let the word of Christ richly dwell within you" (Colossians 3:16). The word must settle down in our lives and make its home in our hearts. Peter writes, "Like newborn babies, long for the pure milk of the word, so that by it you may grow in respect to salvation" (1 Peter 2:2). Such hunger for the word is a mark of a spiritually maturing life.

Your spiritual life is strongest when your desire for the Scriptures is greatest. Does your heart long for the pure milk of the word? What might be stifling your hunger for it? Do you have a spiritual longing in your soul for the truth? Such a holy appetite will produce true joy and authentic godliness in our well-fed souls.

The Confidence of Seeing God at Work

Paul states the purpose for his future release from Roman imprisonment if it should come. He writes, "… so that your proud confidence in me may abound in Christ Jesus through my coming to you again" (Philippians **1:26**). This "proud confidence" of the Philippians toward Paul represents their rejoicing in seeing him again. These two little phrases "in me" and "in Christ Jesus" convey the reality of his Christian life. There are no words between these phrases in the original Greek. Further, the order of what Paul wrote is reversed in this English translation. More correctly, this reads that their proud confidence is "in Christ Jesus in me." The order is important: Christ appears first, and then Paul. The reason they have such confidence in Paul is because of what Christ is doing in him. The apostle does not encourage them to be proud of him simply because of him. Rather, they should have great confidence in what Christ is doing in Paul.

Once Paul is released, they will know that it was the Lord who providentially intervened to bring it to pass. There will be no human explanation for this except that God overruled in this matter. Therefore, when it occurs, all the glory will go to God alone. They will know that the Lord has purposeful plans to use Paul in the lives of the churches. This release will cause their burdened hearts for him to be thrilled. Paul is not wanting to be released in order to escape the difficulty in Rome. Instead, he is willing to stay so that unbelievers may come to know Christ and believers grow closer to him.

We should be able to relate to what the Philippians would be feeling. Our own hearts are encouraged whenever we see God at work in other Christians. This is especially true when we have prayed for them, and we witness the answer to our pleas. It causes our hearts to rejoice as we see God at work in their lives. It is right for us to feel this way because of what God is doing in them.

As we conclude this chapter, I want to ask you a hard question: Are you ready to die? The apostle Paul was prepared for such a departure as he sat in this Roman imprisonment. Are you ready for your time on earth to come to a conclusion, and then to stand before the Lord? There is only one way to be prepared for the reality of that future time. You must put your entire trust in the Lord Jesus Christ.

If you were to taste death today, can you say the same as Paul, that you are ready to be with Christ? If you have never done so, I want to urge you to turn to the Lord, confess your sins, and commit your life to him.

If you have already surrendered your life to Christ, I want to encourage you to live in a way that sees death as gain. It will be through the gates of death that you will enter into the immediate presence of Jesus Christ. But if we live for self, death will be, in some measure, loss—the regret of the life we could and should have lived if only we had lived it wholeheartedly for Christ. Only by living for him, who is the object of our faith and the source of our life, will we be able to say that death is gain.

This must be our heart cry: "To live is Christ and to die is gain." Jesus Christ is the only One for whom life is worth living. Every day, make the purpose of your being to live completely for him. Only then will death be a graduation to glad glory when you stand before him.

Questions for reflection

1. "Will I do what I want to do, or will I do what is best for others?" When in your daily life should you be asking yourself this question—and how will you answer it?

2. Which verse from this section would be most helpful for you to commit to memory, and when do you think you will most need to recall it and live it out?

3. Are you ready to die?

5. GOSPEL COMMITMENT

The High Price of the Free Gift

The gospel is good news of salvation in Jesus Christ and is the greatest announcement that this world has ever heard. It is the glad tidings that this **fallen** human race may find salvation from the wrath of God through the sinless life and **substitutionary** death of Jesus Christ. Jesus obtained perfect righteousness by living the perfect life that we could never live. Further, he purchased our pardon from sin by his death upon the cross, through the shedding of his blood and the giving of his life, and by this sin-bearing, substitutionary act Jesus redeemed all those whom he came to save. Forgiveness of sin is offered to all as a free gift that is received by faith alone apart from any good works.

For those who receive this gospel, though, it always comes at a high price. When anyone believes in Jesus Christ and receives his righteousness and the forgiveness of sin, this act of saving faith requires deep soul-searching and radical self-denial. This step of faith necessitates a supreme commitment to the lordship of Jesus Christ. For those who embrace the gospel, it will cost them everything. It requires a willingness to suffer the opposition of Satan and the persecution of the world. Every true believer must be willing to endure reproach, ridicule, and rejection. A follower of Christ must recognize that all they have belongs to their Master. They must be willing to relinquish their earthly popularity, pleasures, and possessions. A disciple must be willing to receive slander, shame, and suffering for the gospel. This is the high cost of discipleship, and its price is never marked down.

So although the gospel is good news, it is never an easy message to live. Followers of Christ cannot expect better treatment in the world than he himself received. Upon the cross the Lord Jesus paid the supreme price for the salvation he purchased. In a similar manner, those who are born of the Spirit must carry their cross and sacrifice all they are and have for the gospel. This is the reality of believing the good news of Jesus Christ, and it necessitates dying to self in order to live in obedience to Christ.

This is the specific focus of the next few verses in Paul's letter. He now feels a great need to remind the Philippians of the enormous sacrifice they must be willing to pay to be followers of Christ. Likewise, these verses serve as a reminder of the price that every believer in Christ—including you and me—must pay if they are to walk in a manner worthy of their calling.

The Conduct the Gospel Requires

Paul begins this brief paragraph by telling the Philippians that they must live in a manner consistent with the gospel: "Only conduct yourselves in a manner worthy of the gospel of Christ" (**v 27a**). "Only" means they must exclusively live in a manner consistent with the gospel. There is no latitude for them to live in any other manner. They must conduct themselves in a way that honors the gospel and, thus, live distinctly and differently than the world. They must model the message they have now embraced. They entered the kingdom with the surrender of their lives to Jesus Christ. This is precisely how they must live out the reality of their faith.

To live in "a manner worthy of the gospel" is an expression which summarizes all that is required in Christian living. Included in this statement is every teaching and every command in the Bible relevant for New Testament believers. "Conduct yourselves" (*politeuomai*) means to live as the citizen of a country in a law-abiding manner. As Fee points out:

"Paul is here making a play on their 'dual citizenship'—of the empire by virtue of their being Philippians; of heaven by virtue of their faith in Christ and incorporation into the believing community." (*Paul's Letter to the Philippians,* page 161)

Paul is saying that the Philippian believers are under an obligation to live in a way that is consistent with the word of God, which governs his people.

This verb "conduct" needs to be broken down in order to understand what it requires. First, in the Greek "conduct yourselves" is in the **present tense**. This means that they must live every moment of every day in the manner prescribed. Second, this verb is in the **middle voice**, indicating that it is incumbent upon each believer to assume this charge. Third, it is a **second person** plural verb, revealing that this conduct is prescribed for every believer. Fourth, this is in the imperative mood—a command from God himself with binding authority upon their lives. Combining all four of these aspects, Paul is saying, *Live consistent with the gospel always. Take action with this, all of you—and that is God's command.* This command is for everyone, always.

> How we live must be consistent with what we believe; otherwise we will be a walking contradiction in terms.

The implication is that how we live must be consistent with what we believe; otherwise we will be a walking contradiction in terms. A disciple of Christ is responsible for conducting themselves in a way that matches and showcases the gospel they believe. As believers, we must never become passive in pursuing holiness. We must walk in a godly manner of life. Are you a citizen of the kingdom of God, a believer in Christ? If so, this command is directed to you. We must answer this call to "only" conduct ourselves in a manner worthy of the gospel.

The Consistency the Gospel Demands

The Philippians must live consistently with the gospel "so that whether I come and see you or remain absent, I will hear of you that you are standing firm" (**v 27b**). In other words, whether he is present with them or absent, they must live in the same manner. This faithful endurance is so important that Paul will repeat this charge later in the next chapter: "So then, my beloved, just as you have always obeyed, not as in my presence only, but now much more in my absence..." (2:12). Paul makes it clear that his present absence from them did not allow them to become lax in their Christian living. They could not use his separation from them in Rome as an excuse for their spiritual lives to become less than what they should be. God is always present with every believer, whether others are present and watching or not. All believers must live as he requires, regardless of who is present or absent.

This principle is relevant for every believer today. No matter who is with us or not, we must maintain the same devotion to God in consistent obedience to his word. Whether you find yourself in the midst of Christian fellowship or removed from their watching eyes, we must keep the commandments of the Lord with equal resolution. Are you isolated from the observance of your spiritual leaders? Are you a traveling business person away from your circle of Christian friends? Are you removed from the proximity of a disciple or mentor? Are you providentially removed from Christian fellowship? Whatever your situation, an absence from others must never be allowed to be an excuse for becoming spiritually blasé toward keeping the word of God. After all, the One whose verdict matters most is never absent. So when we do find ourselves alone or isolated, we must live consciously *corum deo*—that is, in the presence of God. The Lord is always with us in every place. More importantly, through the Holy Spirit, he lives inside of us with the full sufficiency of his grace. Even when we are separated from family or friends, he gives the divine enablement to keep his word.

Obedience Is Never Optional

What are the particular characteristics required in living lives worthy of the gospel? Paul mentions several ways in which the Philippians must occupy their thoughts. We will consider these in the second half of this chapter. But before we proceed to consider these distinctive marks, let us remember: it matters to God how we live our lives. Grace does not diminish our responsibility to the moral requirements of what God requires. Grace does not lower the standard. Rather, grace enables us to meet it. Grace empowers us to fulfill what God requires.

Obedience to the word is never optional for the Christian. Keeping the commandments of God flows from a heart of love for Jesus Christ. We will examine in the second half of this chapter what this submissive compliance to the word of God means in daily life.

Questions for reflection

1. "Followers of Christ cannot expect better treatment in the world than he himself received." How is this a great encouragement to believers who are suffering for their loyalty to Christ?

2. As you consider your own conduct, in which areas are you encouraged by its consistency with the gospel you believe in? Are there areas in which you are being challenged to change your conduct?

3. Do you ever use being apart from other believers as an excuse not to live in a manner worthy of the gospel? How would remembering that God is never absent change your conduct in those times?

PART TWO

So, what are the ways that Paul calls us to conduct ourselves in a manner that is consistent with the gospel?

1. Stand Together

First, Paul writes that his readers must be "standing firm in one spirit, with one mind striving together for the faith of the gospel" (**v 27c**). "Standing firm" (*steko*) means to be stationary, in a fixed position. The idea is to not be pushed or moved around by another force, but rather, to be anchored in one place. This is a military term that pictures a soldier holding his position on the front lines of battle. If the soldier neglects his post, the enemy can secure the advantage. Hendriksen says that:

> "The unity here envisioned is one of striving or struggling side by side, like gladiators, against a common foe."

(*Philippians*, pages 86-87)

In like manner, the believer must stand in the face of spiritual opposition. The enemies of God look for the weakest soldier in his army. If the foes of God can defeat the weakest soldier, it becomes the entry point to penetrate the church and bring about a devastating defeat.

Both individually and collectively, the Philippians must not be moved away from their allegiance to the gospel. They must stand firm in the faith. They must be anchored in the truth of the apostles' teaching. When confronted by error and sin, they must not be swayed or back down. When persecuted and oppressed, they must not turn and run from their Christian witness. In the midst of spiritual warfare, they must remain immovable in the gospel.

As the Philippians stand together, they must be "in one spirit, with one mind" (**v 27**). "Spirit" (*pneuma*) is the internal power or drive within a person. It is the thing that makes them strive and live and breathe. To be "in one spirit" refers to the unity that must forge together their inner drive. There is strength to be drawn from their common commitment to the gospel. To be of "one mind" is a parallel expression to this, further explaining what "one spirit" means. These two phrases represent the same reality. "Mind" (*psuché*) is the word for psyche, or soul. This conveys the entirety of one's inner soul, including the intellect, affections, and will. So pictured here is the entire inner human life of a person. They must stand firm together with oneness of heart, interlocking arms with one another, posted as one man in their stance for the gospel. They must embrace the same convictions in the truth and hold to the same allegiance to the Lord Jesus Christ.

This summons applies to every believer today. It matters what any group of disciples believe and how they stand strong together in the faith. It is not enough that the leaders of a church stand firm in the truth. Every member in the body of Christ must stand together in the apostles' teaching. Any departure from the word is a departure from Christ himself. The church must stand together in and for the truth of the word.

2. Strive Together

Second, Paul continues to write that the Philippians must be "striving together for the faith of the gospel" (**v 27d**). The main root of the word translated "striving" (*sunathleo*) gives the English language words such as "athlete" and "athletic." The idea pictures someone competing with maximum effort in an athletic contest such as running or wrestling. A **prefix** (*sula*) meaning "with" is added to the front of this verb—the Philippians must contend *with one another* in their witness for Christ in the face of much opposition. They must contend *together* for the Christian faith. They must fight *together* against the world, the flesh, and the devil to live out their convictions in the truth.

Paul explains that this fighting is "for the faith of the gospel," a reference to the objective faith. That is, they must strive for the apostles' teaching (Acts 2:42), "sound doctrine" (Titus 2:1), and "the faith which was once for all handed down to the saints" (Jude 3). Striving together for the Christian faith means they must maintain their unity in the truth. This is not a nebulous unity built upon shallow emotions, but upon "that form of teaching to which you were committed" (Romans 6:17). They must strive for "the whole purpose of God" (Acts 20:27). Their unity must be built upon the rock of divine revelation (Matthew 7:24). They can only advance the good news of Jesus Christ as they strive together as one man.

3. Sanctified Together

Third, Paul adds that his readers should be, "in no way alarmed by your opponents—which is a sign of destruction for them, but of salvation for you, and that too, from God" (Philippians **1:28**). Such resistance was to be expected for followers of Christ. Jesus said it would come: "I chose you out of the world, [and] because of this the world hates you" (John 15:19). Again, Jesus promised, "In the world you have tribulation" (John 16:33). This was affirmed by Paul: "Through many tribulations we must enter the kingdom of God" (Acts 14:22). Likewise, Peter says, "Beloved, do not be surprised at the fiery ordeal among you … as though some strange thing were happening to you" (1 Peter 4:12). Neither should the Philippians be surprised or alarmed by this opposition.

The "opponents" of the Philippian Christians are the false teachers who have infiltrated the church in Philippi with their corrupt teaching. These are the **Judaizers** who attempt to put the Philippians back under the **Mosaic law** of the old covenant. They are "the dogs," unclean and vicious—"evil workers" who teach a "false circumcision" (Philippians 3:2). They are "enemies of the cross of Christ, whose end is destruction" (3:18-19). These false teachers must be exposed and resisted, lest they pollute the body of believers in Philippi and misdirect their lives.

This striving together for the gospel, Paul writes, was a "sign" (**1:28**). Their stance for the gospel was "a sign of destruction" for the false teachers and those who follow their twisted teaching. This speaks of the final judgment and eternal doom for those who pervert the gospel of Jesus Christ. Paul minces no words when he writes, "But even if we, or an angel from heaven, should preach to you a gospel contrary to what we have preached to you, he is to be accursed! As we have said before, so I say again now, if any man is preaching to you a gospel contrary to what you received, he is to be accursed!" (Galatians 1:8-9). Those who preach another gospel are to be damned because with their false gospel they are leading people to damnation.

Further, their contending for the truth "is a sign ... of salvation for you" (Philippians **1:28**). The spiritual adversity that the Philippians are facing in their fight for the faith is a confirming "sign" that they are genuinely converted to Christ. A lack of spiritual oppression may be an indicator of a lack of conversion. If they were not truly converted, they would give in instead of standing firm. Likewise, the opposition is a demonstration to the world of the differences between what they preach and what the Judaizers teach. If they did not stand firm in the gospel against the false teaching of the Judaizers, it would call into question the authenticity of their message of grace. A lack of resilience in the truth would send mixed signals to the world. Further, a lack of opposition to their message would raise the question of where they stand in this spiritual warfare in which they find themselves. But as they stand strong with the other believers in Philippi in the unity in the faith, it is a positive sign of the genuineness of their salvation. Such solidarity brings the assurance that God is at work in their lives.

The final words, "and that too, from God," indicate that the destruction of those who reject the gospel is from God, just as salvation is also from him. How the Philippian believers stood strong in the gospel was a powerful "sign" to the world. The evidence that they were suffering for the truth was bearing a powerful witness to those living in Philippi. A sure indicator of the future destruction in eternity for their opponents was the rejection of the one true gospel. At the same time, this striving for the gospel is a "sign" of the salvation for those who are true believers in Jesus Christ. In times of persecution, it becomes clearer where people stand regarding the gospel. The conflict forces the divide and a deeper commitment to Christ of his authentic disciples.

In the same way, we must accept the suffering that will come as we live out our faith in the gospel. This opposition to the truth is to be expected as a necessary part of our Christian walk. We will be persecuted, in some measure, for our faith. Otherwise, we have not let our witness for Christ be known. Such opposition is a sure sign of our opponents 'destruction and of our salvation.

4. Suffer Together

Paul continues, "For to you it has been granted for Christ's sake ... to believe in Him" (**v 29**). To all believers, saving faith "has been granted." That is, it has been given to them by God "to believe in Him." If anyone is to believe in Christ, it must be given to them by God to believe. No one can believe the gospel on their own. Every unbeliever is spiritually dead in trespasses and sins (Ephesians 2:1). They are a slave of sin and must obey sin. Left to themselves, they will not believe God in his saving message (Romans 3:10-11). In order for anyone to believe in the gospel, God must grant the gift of saving faith. God gives such enabling grace to all whom he chose in eternity past for salvation.

The rest of Scripture teaches that saving faith is a gift from God that he must grant. "For by grace you have been saved through faith; and that not of yourselves, it is the gift of God; not as a result of works, so that no one may boast (Ephesians 2:8-9). "Fixing our eyes on Jesus, the author and perfecter of faith..." (Hebrews 12:2a). "And on the basis of faith in His name, it is the name of Jesus which has strengthened this man whom you see and know; and the faith which comes through Him has given him this perfect health in the presence of you all" (Acts 3:16). "To those who have received a faith of the same kind as ours..." (2 Peter 1:1). Paul tells the Philippians that they must submit together because their faith was granted to them by God.

To all who are given saving faith, God also appoints them "to suffer for His sake" (Philippians **1:29**). Those two gifts—salvation and suffering—are inseparably bound together. This suffering was for the sake of the gospel. It included every believer in the church at Philippi, and not simply the overseers and the deacons (1:1). All who receive the former also receive the latter. These two are a package deal. All the believers in Philippi had been granted saving faith, as well as the privilege of suffering for the gospel. Paul wrote elsewhere, "All who desire to live godly in Christ Jesus will be persecuted" (2 Timothy 3:12). "But to the degree that you share the sufferings of Christ, keep on rejoicing, so that also at the revelation of His glory you may rejoice with exultation. If you are reviled for the name of Christ, you are blessed, because the Spirit of glory and of God rests on you" (1 Peter 4:13-14). Suffering because of our salvation is to be expected and accepted.

When Paul adds, "for His sake" (Philippians **1:29**), he refers to suffering specifically for the gospel. Spiritual conflict with the forces of darkness is the inevitable result of being publicly identified with Christ and his gospel. Saving faith is a gift from God, and so also is suffering for the gospel. This truth sounds strange to the world, but not so strange to genuine believers. Jesus himself suffered to purchase salvation at the cost of his own life. He said that the slave cannot expect better treatment than his master (Matthew 10:24). If people hated Christ, they will hate his disciples. In an argument from the greater to the lesser, if they persecuted Jesus Christ, they will persecute all who believe in him. To suffer for Christ, as to be saved by Christ, is a blessing:

> Suffering because of our salvation is to be expected and accepted.

"The double blessing is this: on behalf of Christ, not only to believe in Him but also to suffer on his behalf."

(Hendriksen, *Philippians,* page 90)

5. Struggle Together

Paul concludes this paragraph by encouraging the believers in Philippi that they are "experiencing the same conflict which you saw in me" (Philippians **1:30**). The word "conflict" (*agon*) means "agony." It was a term representing the painful effort expended by athletes in the arena of the stadium where the athletic contests were held. It was where the runners, wrestlers, and boxers suffered great pain in competition. Athletes pushed themselves to the limit until their bodies were often black and blue. Later, this word came to be used for the marathon, that grueling 26-mile race. Subsequently, it came to be identified with the athletic stadium in which the ancient games were held, such as in Rome and outside Corinth. It would also be in similar stadiums that the Christians would be fed to the lions. Paul is talking not about a brief or superficial pain, but a deep agony.

Amid their godless culture, the Philippians are in the fight for the gospel. Paul writes to these believers who are experiencing this conflict for their faith so that they will be encouraged as they are facing stiff opposition. He himself is imprisoned in Rome in chains for the gospel as he writes these words. The Philippians are fighting the same fight as him. They are running the same race and waging the same war. Persecution is not always to the same degree with every believer, but it is a reality for all who follow Christ.

After all, Paul reminds the Philippian Christians, "you saw in me" the suffering that comes to the saved (**v 30**). He is referring to the affliction he suffered in Philippi. When Paul came to Philippi on his second missionary journey (Acts 16), he brought the gospel to a small gathering of women at the local riverside. Beginning with a woman named Lydia, people were converted, and their conversions to Christ set off a firestorm of persecution. Due to the gospel, Paul was arrested, mobbed, and beaten. He was imprisoned and put into stocks. The Philippians saw this conflict with their own eyes. Paul is reminding them of this to encourage them. He has already suffered, and so have they. Their suffering for the gospel puts them in good company with him.

And it continues through life—so that the Philippians "now hear [this suffering] to be in me." Four times in his first chapter, Paul refers to his "imprisonment" in Rome for the gospel (Philippians 1:7, 13, 14, 17). He points to the possibility of his "death" because of this message (v 20). He states he is ready "to die" for the truth (v 21). At the end of this letter, he will talk about his "affliction" (4:14). The Philippians have repeatedly heard about adversity from Paul in this letter. They have also heard about Paul's suffering from Epaphroditus, their pastor, who sat with Paul to comfort him. In the process, Epaphroditus almost died due to the hard demands of the strenuous travel involved in coming to Rome. Paul sent him back to the Philippians, which is how this letter was put into their hands. As Epaphroditus read this letter to the church, they heard about the imprisonment and afflictions of Paul. Epaphroditus surely gave a careful description of the condition and sacrifices suffered by the apostle in this house arrest.

What Paul wrote to the church at Philippi has come down through the centuries to us. The only differences are the name of the church where you worship and the city in which you live. However, the message is the same. Nothing has changed. Paul says to all believers everywhere that living for the gospel necessitates suffering for the gospel. Salvation and suffering cannot be divorced, and we must not live our lives as though the Bible's teaching on this does not apply to us in our age or stage or society. We are not to be needlessly offensive, but we are to speak and live out the truth in love. As we do, we must understand that there will always be a price to pay in proclaiming the message. The gospel is good news, but it is never easy news. It is a demanding call to repentance and faith that requires a full sacrifice from each one of us. But but it is worth the sacrifice we make, because it is the gospel that saves, and it is a redeemed life that advances that gospel into the world.

> The gospel is good news, but it is never easy news.

Questions for reflection

1. How can you contribute to your church:
   - standing together?
   - striving together?
   - being a sign together?
   - suffering together?
   - struggling together?

2. What difference does it make that all these things are to be done together as church, rather than primarily or only individually?

3. "The gospel is good news, but it is never easy news." How does the content of the gospel motivate you to live out the gospel?

6. A HIGH CALL TO A LOWLY LIFE

The Christian life is full of opposites that seem to contradict themselves. We must die to self if we would live for Christ. We must declare spiritual bankruptcy if we would be rich. We must mourn if we would be happy. We must hunger if we would be satisfied. We must lose our life if we would save it, but if we save our life we will lose it.

But perhaps the greatest apparent contradiction is what we have before us in this chapter: *We must humble ourselves if we are to be exalted.*

"Humility" is a word that means to think or to judge ourselves with lowliness. The idea is for someone "not to think more highly of himself than he ought to think; but to think so as to have sound judgment" (Romans 12:3). It is sometimes said that "Humility is one of those things that if you think you have it, you don't." Humility, in the truest sense of the word, is a central **tenet** of the Christian faith.

The Greeks, however, did not even have a word for humility, because it was considered of such a low value. The concept was entirely foreign to the Greeks and utterly abhorrent to the Romans. The word for humility was coined when the church was birthed. Some speculate that the word was even invented by Paul himself in writing these verses.

For a believer, humility is the most foundational of all Christian virtues. No one struts through the narrow gate that leads into the kingdom. No one high-steps their way down the narrow path. We are sheep, not peacocks; servants, not sovereigns. If Christ is to fill our lives, we must empty ourselves. If Christ is to increase, we must decrease. Paul wrote to the Colossian church, "As you have received Christ Jesus the Lord, so walk in Him" (Colossians 2:6). We received him in humility. Therefore, we must walk in ever-increasing humility. The more we mature spiritually, the more humble we must become.

This virtue of humility is the central theme that runs through Philippians 2:1-11. The actual word "humility" is found in **verse 3**, but the concept is seen throughout this entire section. Paul calls upon the believers in Philippi to put on humility (**v 3**) as they carry out their ministry (**v 4**) in order to preserve their unity (**v 1-2**). In order to show us how to do so, the apostle will point to the Lord Jesus Christ as the supreme example in understanding true humility (**v 5-11**).

An Appeal for Certainty

Before Paul exhorts the Philippians to humility, he first reminds them of the certainty of grace in their lives: "Therefore if there is any encouragement in Christ, if there is any consolation of love, if there is any fellowship of the Spirit, if any affection and compassion" (**v 1**). The word "if" is found four times in this opening verse of this new section. Each time, it can equally accurately be translated as "since" or "because." So this verse could be rendered, "Because there is encouragement in Christ," or "Since there is encouragement in Christ." Paul is making a statement of fact. His assertion implies an affirmative in response. There is much encouragement in the person and work of Christ.

"Encouragement" (*paraklesis*) means a calling near, or a coming alongside another in order to help. Jesus Christ left heaven in order that he might come alongside believers to help them in their Christian life. The encouragement and the consolation of Christ is given by the ministry of the Holy Spirit, who indwells believers. By his Spirit, in times of greatest discouragement, the Lord Jesus Christ himself lifts up hearts and strengthens faith. In times of greatest despair and despondency, Jesus comes alongside his people and speaks words of hope and comfort. Even in the darkest hours, he pours joy into trembling hearts. Jesus has poured his all-sufficient peace into our depleted souls.

Paul next states, "if [or because, or since] there is any consolation of love..." The word "consolation" means the comfort and solace of the trembling heart. It is a **synonym** for "encouragement" used in the previous line—so we can add "in Christ" after the word "love," just as it has already appeared after "encouragement." There is an unlimited supply of consolation in Christ for every believer in him.

Next Paul adds, "if there is any fellowship of the Spirit." "Fellow-ship" (*koinania*) means partnership between people. The word was used of business partners who were involved together in the same venture. The Christian always has the active participation of the Spirit in them, bringing the encouragement of Jesus Christ to the depths of their soul. Jesus sent the Holy Spirit to be "another Comforter" (John 14:16, see footnote) to bring to believers the supernatural peace of Christ that only he can give.

Paul concludes his "if" clauses with, "if any affection and compassion" (Philippians **2:1**) Once again, "in Christ" and "of the Spirit" are to be presumed at the end of this line. This deep affection and tender compassion are found exclusively in Jesus Christ, and are poured into Christians' hearts by the Spirit. The Holy Spirit causes the abundant blessings of Christ to be experienced by all whom he indwells. This affection and compassion of Christ is experienced by every believer, albeit in varying degrees. Within every Christian, there is an ever-increasing triumph and abundant supply of each one of these conditions that we read about in **verse 1**.

Has the Lord brought you encouragement when you have been downcast? Has his fellowship been real when others have forsaken you and you have felt all alone? Has his consolation elevated your spirit and picked up your heart? Praise God for the times you can look back to and about which you can say "yes"; and pray that these realities might be more and more the realities of your experience, and the realities that you rest upon.

An Appeal for Unity

Based upon this sturdy foundation, Paul now appeals for unity among the believers in Philippi: "Make my joy complete by being of the same mind, maintaining the same love, united in spirit, intent on one purpose" (**v 2**). The joy of the apostle will be enlarged as the Philippians live in unity with one another. It is Paul's desire that the Philippians stand as one body by making no distinctions between themselves. They must love one another with the same love that they have for each and every member in the church.

Of course, they will be relationally closer to some believers than they are to others. This may be, for example, because of common traits or life experiences that they share. Or it could be as a result of similar interests. But, Paul says, they must have the same love for one another. The love they show must be the same for all.

The Philippians will bring further joy to Paul's heart as they are "united in spirit." Hendriksen points out that...

"This is Paul's deep concern. Not speedy release from prison but the spiritual progress of the Philippians—of all of them—is his chief desire." (*Philippians,* page 99)

> Christians should be one-souled, welded together with a common acceptance of each other.

The word "united" here means to be "one-souled." This requires that their spirits should be knitted together with mutual love for Christ and living in harmony with one another. Christians should be one-souled—their souls should be welded together with a common acceptance of each other. He further adds that they must be "intent on one purpose." Though not stated, this one purpose is their common pursuit of the glory of God (v 11; 4:20). They must be collectively pursuing the exaltation of Christ as the chief focus of their lives.

An Appeal for Humility

Paul now makes his appeal for humility. He makes two negative instructions (**2:3a, 4a**), each followed with a positive assertion (**v 3b, 4b**). He begins, "Do nothing from selfishness or empty conceit" (**v 3**). Paul is saying that the Philippians must do nothing in a contentious manner. "Selfishness" (*epitheia*) means a fractious spirit that produces strife. It is the idea of the kind of self-seeking and self-promoting attitude that creates, or even seeks and enjoys, divisions. It is wrong for them to elevate themselves above others with a self-promoting spirit. Pride exalts self above the glory of God and the good of others. But being a Christian means that we must die daily to self (Luke 9:23).

Stating it positively, Paul continues, "But with humility of mind regard one another as more important than yourselves" (Philippians **2:3**). The Philippians cannot humble themselves under the Lord if they are simultaneously seeking to elevate themselves over others. To put it another way, to humble themselves before one another must start with them surrendering to the lordship of Jesus Christ. Humility begins with your mindset. "Humility of mind" is the complete opposite of self-exaltation and the **antithesis** of pride.

When Paul tells his readers to "regard" one another with a lowly mindset, he uses a word taken from the ancient world of mathematics, meaning "to calculate." This stresses that they must count or calculate one another as more important than themselves. They must add up the needs of others, at the same time subtracting their personal interests. They must arrive at a bottom-line summary of what would most benefit others, and then act upon the result of that calculation.

The Interests of Others

Paul restates this with a further negative and a further positive assertion: "Do not merely look out for your own personal interests, but also for the interests of others" (**v 4**). He is wanting to stress that the believer must take the same concern that they have for themselves and apply it to others.

To "look out for" others means to keep an eye out for their needs. We must be on the alert for the welfare of others. We should be sharp in our focus upon the needs of others. We must not live without regard for others. If we as believers are primarily focused upon God and his glory, we will automatically be concerned for serving the needs of others, especially those in his family.

Everything in our Christian lives is designed to produce a greater humility in us. The word of God sanctifies us, promoting humility as a mindset. The cross tells us that all we bring to our salvation is our sin. It is impossible to enter the Christian life with pride! Prayer puts us on our knees before God with empty hands. Worship causes us to look up to God, which puts us in our proper place. Our trials humble us, reminding us of our human frailty. And yet despite all this, our hearts still struggle not to feel proud. Our default position is to exalt ourselves, despite all the evidence that there is nothing about which we should be proud. So, we need to take Paul's words here to heart. Just as he stated them to the Philippians for their growth, so we need to affirm them to ourselves for our own growth today. Since we have all the encouragement and consolation and fellowship of Christ through his Spirit, we should see others not as opportunities to bring glory to ourselves, but as people we can serve in order to bring glory to Christ. Since we know the affection and compassion of Christ, we must aim to calculate others' interests and needs as far above our own as our Savior did for us.

Questions for reflection

1. What is your instinctive reaction to the word "humility"?

2. Has reading this section changed your definition of humility, or your appreciation of it, in any way?

3. How can you look to the interests of others more than your own today?

PART TWO

The Supreme Example

Where do we look to see humility worked out in life? To establish his point, Paul points the Philippians to the supreme example of humility: the Lord Jesus Christ himself. No greater model could be given than this: "Have this attitude in yourselves which was also in Christ Jesus" (**v 5**).

Paul is referring to the mindset that he is exhorting the Philippians to have. He is not concerned with a merely outward religious façade. Paul is probing into the depths of their spiritual life when he requires this kind of self-denying attitude. Humility is clearly seen in the entrance of Christ into this world. God does not ask anything of these believers that he did not ask of his own Son, Jesus Christ. When the apostle writes that Christ "humbled Himself" (**v 8**), he shows the steps downward that Christ took from the heights of heaven into the depths of this world.

The greatest display of humility that the world has ever witnessed was the incarnation of Christ, which led ultimately to his crucifixion. Here Jesus demonstrated what it looks like to truly be humble. He himself declared that he "did not come to be served, but to serve, and to give His life a ransom for many" (Mark 10:45). From a sovereign to a servant—this was the lowly role that Jesus assumed.

As Paul describes this state of mind, he starts with Jesus at the highest level. He begins by asserting the full deity of Jesus Christ: "He existed in the form of God" (Philippians **2:6**). From eternity past, Jesus was fully and truly divine. From before time began, he has always possessed all of the divine perfections that belong to God alone. Jesus was in the form of God from before the foundation of the world. The divine perfections that have belonged to the Father are also the eternal possession of the Son. Jesus Christ, the Son of God, is co-equal and co-eternal with God the Father.

And yet, Paul writes, the Son of God "did not regard equality with

God a thing to be grasped." Jesus did not cling to the full exercise of the **prerogatives** of his deity. He did not clutch his rights as God, but chose to obey the will of the Father.

The Supreme Selflessness

The first step down in the self-humiliation of Jesus Christ was when he "emptied Himself, taking the form of a bond-servant, and being made in the likeness of men" (**v 7**). "Emptied" (*kenoo*) means "abased." What is described here is not Jesus emptying himself of his eternal deity. Nor does it mean that Jesus exchanged his deity for humanity. Rather, this asserts that he laid aside his prerogatives as God in order to take on the limitations of humanity. The Son of God added to his person a human nature without surrendering any of his divine attributes. This was an act of self-renunciation on the part of the Son of God by which he voluntarily chose not to exercise all his rights as God during the time of his earthly life. But at no time did he rid himself of any divine perfections. Calvin helpfully describes Paul's teaching this way:

> "[Jesus] had been brought down to the level of mankind, so that there was in appearance nothing that differed from the common condition of mankind."
>
> (*The Epistles of Paul to the Galatians, Ephesians, Philippians and Colossians,* page 58)

We need to linger here, in order to appreciate and marvel at this. In his incarnation, Jesus did not diminish in his deity. When he assumed human flesh, he never became less than fully God. What Jesus did yield was the free exercise of his divine prerogatives. He likewise sacrificed the intimate relationship he had enjoyed with the Father from eternity past. While taking upon himself sinless humanity, he remained fully God; but he surrendered every advantage as God. He chose to empty himself of the constant use of his deity.

The Supreme Servant

The coming of the second Person of the eternal Trinity into the human race involved him "taking the form of a bond-servant" (**v 7**). He did not come as royalty in shining majesty. Jesus came as a "bond-servant" (*doulos*).

"Form" (*morphe*) is used twice in this verse and is a different word than was used in the previous verse. It means "existing as," or "possessing the status of." He assumed the position of a slave, which was far more humbling than being a servant. A servant was hired to accomplish a specific task, but retained certain rights. A slave had a lower status. He belonged to his master and owned no personal property. He had no life of his own, apart from the will of his master. Jesus assumed the form of a slave. There was no lower position for him to occupy. John MacArthur writes that…

"Jesus served others more completely than any other servant or
slave who has ever lived." (*The MacArthur New Testament
Commentary on Philippians,* page 129)

This is what it means that Jesus was "being made in the likeness of men" (**v 7**). Jesus, the Son of God, assumed all of the limitations of finite humanity. While he remained fully and truly God, he became fully and truly man. Like any other person, Jesus grew weary and tired. He hungered and thirsted. He felt all of the throbbing pain of a human body. He subjected himself to the indignities of human pressures, temptations, and sufferings. Paul will reiterate this fact in the next verse: that Jesus was

> The Son of God assumed all of the limitations of finite humanity.

"found in appearance as a man" (**v 8**). He is keen to stress and repeat this truth because it is foundational, wonderful, and awesome. It should move us to praise and joy. Your God is the God who walked this earth as a man.

The Supreme Shame

But that is not all, for "He humbled Himself by becoming obedient to the point of death, even death on a cross" (**v 8**). Jesus came into this world knowing full well that it would end with an ignominious death. Jesus would not die peacefully in his sleep. Rather, he would suffer the worst of all deaths, the dreaded torturous death by crucifixion. He was subjected to the most gruesome kind of death known to the ancient world.

This was a death so loathsome that it was reserved only for the worst criminals. Crucifixion was so despised that Roman law forbade any Roman citizen to be subjected to such cruel treatment. Yet the divine man, Jesus, would be put to death by being nailed to a Roman cross. There he would hang naked, publicly exposed, viewed as an enemy of the empire, condemned as a blasphemer against God.

More than that, Jesus submitted to having the sins of all who would believe in him laid upon him. He who knew no sin became sin for his people (2 Corinthians 5:21). He suffered the full curse of the law (Galatians 3:13), which is death (Romans 6:23). He bore our sins in his body upon the cross (1 Peter 2:24). He shed his blood and took away the sins of all whom the Father would entrust to him (John 1:29; 6:37).

Here is Calvin again:

"Even this was great humility—that from being Lord he became a servant; but [Paul] says that he went farther than this, because, while he was not only immortal, but the Lord of life and death, he nevertheless became obedient to his Father, even so far as to endure death. This was extreme abasement, especially when we take into view the kind of death … For by dying in this manner, he was not only covered with ignominy in the sight of God, but was also accursed in the sight of God."

(The Epistles of Paul to the Galatians, Ephesians, Philippians and Colossians, pages 58-59)

Paul is pointing to the ultimate example of humility. No one ever humbled him-self or herself more than the Lord Jesus Christ. No one ever started so high and no one ever descended so low. No one ever gave up so much as he did (John 15:13). On this basis, the apostle exhorts every believer to be like Christ and lower themselves into humility before God and others.

If he did it, how can you and I not be willing? What right have we to refuse when the One with every right to refuse did not? Every believer must clothe himself with the common rags of servanthood. We must make whatever sacrifice is necessary for the good

> None of us can ever humble ourselves too much.

of others. Given this example, none of us can ever humble ourselves too much. None of us will ever surpass the humility that Christ has demonstrated here. None of us may ever say, "Enough. I deserve better, so I will stop here."

The Supreme Exaltation

Following the humiliation of Christ came his exaltation. Paul writes, "For this reason also, God highly exalted Him, and bestowed on Him the name which is above every name" (Philippians **2:9**). God did not merely exalt him, but highly exalted him. God resurrected his Son from the grave, raising him from the dead. God exalted him above the earth in his ascension. God exalted him above the angels in his coronation. God exalted him to his right hand in the glory above.

On the day of Pentecost, Peter quoted Psalm 110:1, declaring, "The LORD said to my Lord, sit at My right hand, until I make Your enemies a footstool for Your feet" (Acts 2:34). Following his resurrection and ascension, Jesus was exalted to the right hand of the Father, the place of highest authority and honor.

The point is that no one ever truly humbles themselves before God without being exalted by God, whether in this life or in the life to come. True humility will never be forgotten by God. God will see it, God will note it, and God will reward it. It is one thing to be exalted by man, but it is something else entirely, and eternally, to be exalted by God. This is the essence of true humility—to accept that it is our status before God which is of ultimate importance.

There is no higher name that can be conferred upon the Son than the name that the Father gives. Paul will tell us what this name is in **verse 11**—but first comes **verse 10**...

The Supreme Submission

Paul states the purpose of this exaltation: "... so that at the name of Jesus *every knee will bow*, of those who are in heaven and on earth and under the earth" (**v 10**—my italics). Bowing is a sign of submission to a higher authority. It indicates the surrender of the lesser to one who is greater. Do not miss who will one day bow. It includes "those who are in heaven." It includes every elect angel and glorified saint in heaven throughout all the ages. It encompasses those "on earth"—all those in this life, both rescued and rebels, and Satan, who prowls about the earth as a roaring lion (1 Peter 5:8). And it includes all those "under the earth." This is a reference to damned souls already imprisoned and demon spirits already consigned to the pit of hell. As Christ is exalted by God, so too will his name be exalted as well.

The Supreme Confession

On the last day, "every tongue will confess that Jesus Christ is Lord, to the glory of God the Father" (Philippians **2:11**). Here "every tongue" parallels "every knee" in the previous verse. What every tongue will confess is the lordship of Jesus Christ. This means far more than merely stating the word "Lord." Instead, this involves the sober realization of the supremacy of Christ. The word "confess" means to acknowledge; to make an open declaration. This is not a confession that will be mumbled but will be declared. "Lord" (*kurios*) means "Master," "Ruler," "Sovereign," "Supreme One." "Lord" is the name that is above every name, the title of Supreme Ruler over all, the name mentioned earlier (**v 9**). "Jesus" is his earthly name; "Christ" is his messianic title. The Lord Jesus Christ is the One before whom every knee will bow and every tongue will confess.

At the moment of their conversion, everyone who truly believes confesses the lordship of Christ. No one steps through the narrow gate leading to life until they surrender to the lordship of Jesus Christ. In the final judgment, every unconverted person will also confess the lordship of Christ. On the last day, unbelievers will acknowledge that Christ is exactly who he claimed to be: the Son of God and the Son of Man. Every evil spirit and Satan himself will also confess the lordship of Jesus Christ. This universal recognition will be given "to the glory of God the Father" (**v 11**). In the end, Jesus Christ will receive glory from the entire created order. No affirmation of his sovereign deity will be withheld from him.

If we desire to bring glory to God the Father, then we must confess the lordship of Jesus Christ and submit our will to his sovereign will. As we humble ourselves before Christ, we bring greater honor to God the Father. As we live our Christian lives, we must become increasingly more like Jesus Christ. We must live with humility of mind. We must lower ourselves under the mighty hand of God. There must be a death to self at our entrance into the kingdom of God. We must also walk in humility with the Lord daily. We must die to self and seek first the kingdom of God every day that God gives us life, and as we do, we will be exemplifying the mind of Christ.

I have seen this humility of mind when, as a pastor, I have called upon a dying saint in a hospital room. There are often two groups of family members in the room. On one side of the bed is a group that cannot accept this death. They are often an angry group, cursing the doctors and threatening to sue the hospital; or they are despairing, vocally empty of hope. Their failure to accept God's sovereign will is heard loudly.

On the other side of the room is a quiet gathering of people huddled in prayer. These are believers who are giving thanks to God for the salvation of this one who is on death's doorstep. They are humbly resolved to accept the plan of God for their loved one, painful though it may be. Their submission to the will of God reveals their lowliness of mind, like that of their Lord Jesus Christ. And—in such a room and in every other moment of our lives—this is the humility of mind we are to pursue, to grow in, and to display.

Questions for reflection

1. How does reflecting on Christ's humility move you to worship him?

2. How does it challenge you to live like him? Are there times when you say, "Enough. I deserve better, so I will stop here"?

3. What will it look like for you humbly to submit to the will of God in your life right now? How does the gospel enable you to do this gladly, rather than grudgingly?

7. SANCTIFICATION 101

Every one of us always needs to be reinforced in the basics of Christian living. We never grow spiritually beyond this. This involves the understanding of what the Bible calls "sanctification." This is the biblical and theological word which means the divine act of making the believer increasingly holy on a practical level. This pursuit of holiness represents the lifelong process of making a person's moral condition come into conformity with their legal status before God of being "justified." Sanctification is God's continuing work in the believer, who is justified through the power of the Holy Spirit.

The Philippians were no different. They needed a crash course in the elementary principles of spiritual growth. Even the most mature among them had not advanced beyond their need of being further grounded in the elementary truths of Christian living. This next section is an important passage on this critical subject because it deals with the matter of spiritual growth over the duration of our Christian lives. To put it a different way, it answers these questions: *Once I am saved by faith in Christ, what happens next? What takes place in my Christian life after being saved and before going to heaven?* In these verses, the matter of our growth in personal holiness is concisely and precisely explained to us.

To this point, the apostle Paul has stated that for him "to live is Christ" (1:21), and has urged his readers to "conduct [themselves] in a manner worthy of the gospel" (1:27). However, the question remains: How do they live for Christ? How do they live in a manner worthy of their calling? How do they experience growth in their Christian life?

What Paul provides in these verses is one of the finest concise treatments on sanctification to be found in the Bible. These words are succinct, but potent in what they teach on the subject of spiritual growth. Here we have the necessary balance in Christian living between our part (**2:12**) and God's part (**v 13**), followed by some specifics in how this will be evidenced (v 14-18).

The Path of Obedience

Paul begins this section, "So then, my beloved" (**v 12a**). This is addressed exclusively to Christians. Not a word applies to unbelievers. If we miss this point, it will lead us to falsely see these verses as teaching that someone must work to earn their salvation. However, this charge is not delivered to unbelievers, but to "my beloved." This is a clear reference to those who are in the circle of the redeeming love of God. God has a general, benevolent love for all mankind, but a special, specific love for believers. Although God gives general expressions of his **common grace**, he reserves a special love for his own elect, far deeper than his general love for all mankind. This is why Paul addresses the Philippians, as "the beloved." Unbelievers are never referred to in this manner.

Paul continues, "just as you have always obeyed." Obedience to the word of God is the clearly-marked path upon which sanctification moves forward. Every step in the Christian life is to be marked by the truth of the word. Any step of disobedience is a departure from the revealed will of God. From the moment of their conversion, the Philippians were committed to keeping the commandments of God. Paul notes that they "have always obeyed." Theirs was a habitual lifestyle of obedience to the word. This is not meant to imply perfect obedience in any believer. That is impossible. Rather, this indicates a new desire to obey from a new heart that increasingly pursues obedience. In this sense, when they first believed the Philippians immediately "obeyed" as they began living under the authority of the lordship of Jesus Christ.

Paul explains that their obedience has been "not as in my presence only, but now much more in my absence." This is to say, Paul recognizes that he does not have to be in Philippi, at their side, in order for them to live their Christian lives effectively. Their primary dependence is not on Paul, but on the Lord Jesus Christ. The Philippians cannot use the absence of Paul as an excuse that they do not need, or that it is too hard, to obey the Lord. Though Paul is away from them, he commends them for "always" walking in obedience to God. These Philippians believers began walking in the word when Paul was with them and have continued now he is gone. Though he is not with them now, they must continue down that path of obedience.

As a Christian, the same path of obedience has been set before you in your life. Being a believer who is saved by God's grace does not negate your responsibility to keep God's moral law, outlined in his word. There may be times when you will be without the level of spiritual support from older Christians that you enjoyed when you first came to faith, or from those whom you have come to rely upon in your walk of faith; but as with the Philippians, this is not an excuse for compromising on your obedience. When you were born again, God removed your old heart of stone, which was spiritually hardened toward the word, and implanted within you a new heart of flesh that is alive and responsive to his rule and his commands (Ezekiel 36:25-27). Further, God put his Spirit within you, wrote his law upon your heart, and caused you to walk in obedience to his word.

> Being saved by God's grace does not negate your responsibility to keep God's law.

A firm, uncompromising commitment to obeying the word, accompanied by true, serious repentance when you fail, are two marks of a true believer who has been born again (1 John 2:3-6). Do you see this in your life?

Personal Responsibility

In pursuing obedience, Paul urges the Philippians to "work out your salvation" (Philippians **2:12b**). They are commanded to put effort into achieving their salvation. In the Bible, "salvation" is represented in three different ways: as past, present, and future. These three designations involve justification, sanctification, and **glorification**. In justification, believers are saved immediately from the penalty of sin. In sanctification, they are saved progressively from the power and practice of sin. In glorification, they are saved ultimately from the presence of sin. The mention of "salvation" in this verse points to their sanctification in daily Christian living. They were not to work for their salvation, but to work out their salvation. They were to work out what God had already worked in.

In writing the word "work," Paul uses an imperative verb that carries the force of a divine command. These words mean to work thoroughly at something; to take pains in laboring at it. This means that we must expect to expend energy in growing spiritually. Hendriksen puts it this way:

"Their salvation is a process ... in which they themselves, far from remaining passive or dormant, take a very active part. It is a pursuit, a following after, a pressing on, a contest, fight, race."

(*Philippians,* page 120)

This is far removed from a passive **quietist** approach to Christian living—the approach of "let go and let God." Instead, every believer must exert effort in his or her pursuit of holiness. Spiritual couch potatoes grow little in grace or holiness. Being in prayer, studying the Bible, and then obeying it in your life require serious work. Every believer must resist temptation (James 4:7) and discipline themselves for godliness (1 Timothy 4:7-8).

This command applies to every believer. No matter where you are in your spiritual journey, you must work hard at your growth in grace. Are you expending the energy necessary in your pursuit of personal holiness? Are you exercising your spiritual muscles in buffeting your body (1 Corinthians 9:27)? Such is necessary in order to advance in spirituality.

The Joy of Fear and Trembling

Since working out our salvation does require hard work on our part, what will motivate us to perform this labor, and to keep doing so over the days and months and years that may well lie between today and the day of our glorification? There are many motivations, but Paul here mentions just one. Sanctification must be carried out "with fear and trembling" (Philippians **2:12**)—out of a reverential awe for God.

"Fear" (*phobos*) means terror, dread, alarm, reverence. This is not the dread of a ninety-eight pound weakling when he sees the neighborhood bully approaching. Rather, it is wholesome, healthy reverential awe for God and a sober realization of the need to take him seriously. This is often downplayed today as a legitimate motive for Christian living, but it was not so with Paul. This is a soul-gripping fear that grips them to the point of "trembling" (*tromos*). This word indicates a quaking with fear. The phrase carries the idea of a Christian doing his utmost to fulfill his duty, because he knows to whom he owes that duty. In this case, the responsibility is to work out our sanctification with "trembling."

Note that this "fear and trembling" is recorded in a letter that continually emphasizes joy in Christian living. The gladness that believers experience in the Lord grows out of the fertile soil of fearing God with reverential awe. The Philippians were to be sincerely earnest in their Christian life. There was to be nothing casual in their approach to pursuing holiness. God is not a kindly spiritual grandfather, sitting in the sky. God is not a teddy bear. God is not a kitten. God is a lion who loves us, but his love does not mean we are at liberty to domesticate him. Because of this, we are called to tremble joyfully in our walk with God.

Divine Activity

Paul now turns to the other side of the coin of sanctification. He moves from human responsibility to the divine activity within a believer: "for it is God who is at work in you" (**v 13**). "God" refers to God the Father, the first Person of the Trinity. The Father is represented here as the primary agent in the Philippians' sanctification. The Father has sent the Holy Spirit to conform all believers to the image of his Son. The Father uses his word to prune his people for greater fruitfulness (John 15:3). The Father had begun a good work in them at conversion and will continue to work in them throughout the whole of their spiritual growth (Philippians 1:6).

The word "work" is in the present tense, indicating that God is continually active in a Christian's life. God never ceases from his sanctifying ministry in us. God is constantly engaged in producing holiness in every Christian life. Though it will not always feel like God is at work in our life, God nevertheless is always at work within the inner beings of his people. God is relentlessly bringing about spiritual maturity. He is not passive, but dynamic in actively producing their sanctification. Gordon Fee describes how God works and how we work like this:

"This verb [i.e. "work"], as elsewhere, does not so much mean that God is doing it for them, but that God supplies the necessary empowering … Their obedience is ultimately something God effects in/among them … Not only does God empower their 'doing'… but also the 'willing' that lies behind the doing"
(*Paul's Letter to the Philippians,* pages 237-238)

When Paul notes, "For it is God who is at work in you" (**v 13**), the "you" refers to "the beloved" mentioned in the previous verse. This includes every true believer. God is not at work in only a few of the Philippians. Instead, this inner working of daily grace is operative in every true Christian. Moreover, God is at work "in" you—that is, at the deepest level of a person's being. This is not a superficial work that merely addresses the façade of a person's life. Instead, this is a penetrating work at the deepest level of a person's existence.

God was actively engaged in them, Paul indicates, "both to will and to work." The idea is that God's will takes the initiative and is acting upon their will. The divine work in them is what is causing them to work in sanctification. The soul of each believer is the field of labor of this sanctifying work. It is God who is working in them, bringing a gracious force to bear upon their wills.

The Pleasure of God

God is at work in the sanctification of believers "for His good pleasure" (**v 13**). He is actively engaged because he is absolutely holy, and in his people he loves holiness and hates sin. God does this sanctifying work because he loves to cultivate purity of mind, heart, and character in his children. As a father seeks to encourage, exhort and discipline his children to live by the standards of his family, so God nurtures that which conforms to his own nature. It brings great pleasure to God to see his people grow in personal holiness. It delights God to see his image restored in his people.

So working out our own sanctification should bring great pleasure to us as well. It is restoring us to be the people we ought to be, and long to be. The truth that it brings pleasure to our Father in heaven is the reason why the fear and trembling within us is joined with an inner pleasure and joy in the pursuit of godliness. God works to effect our obedience because our keeping his word pleases him. The **corollary** is likewise true. Disobedience displeases God. The exhortation of the apostle Paul to the Philippians is the same exhortation for us today. Let us pursue the holiness that pleases God.

Questions for reflection

1. What effort are you putting into growing spiritually?

2. How can a Christian both enjoy knowing God, and tremble about that same God?

3. How have you been motivated to enjoy growing in sanctification? In which areas in particular will you pray for God to work in you as you work at growing in godliness?

PART TWO

Do Not Grumble

Building upon his foundational teaching on sanctification (v 12-13), Paul now gives us some specific application for daily living. He first addresses the use of the mouth: "Do all things without grumbling or disputing" (**v 14**). The emphasis Paul makes is upon everything a believer does.

The "all things" that the Christian is to "do" is a broad, all-inclusive statement that encompasses all things that God calls us to do in our lives—at home, work, school, church, and play, and in all areas of marriage, parenting, friendship, and ministry. There is nothing in our lives that is not included in this phrase.

In the midst of all their difficulties, even while living in a pagan culture, the Philippians must do all things "without grumbling or disputing." "Grumbling" (*goggasmos*) means murmuring or muttering. The idea is of a secret displeasure not openly spoken about. It refers to private complaining under one's breath. "Disputes" (*dialogismos*) speaks of arguing and debating. It is the product of a contentious spirit that feels the need to be continually questioning what is done in the church. At the same time, this does not imply that a church member could never ask a question or raise a concern. The issue is the attitude of the heart and the tone of the voice.

How easy it is to fall prey to what Paul forbids here. Each one of us must set a guard over our hearts as we live our Christian lives. Murmuring with other believers is a destructive assault upon the unity of the body of Christ. Disputing tears apart what God has joined together. As we become aware of violating this imperative, we must be swift to confess it as sin and repent. We must turn away from this and move in the opposite direction. An anthem of praise must always replace the sour note of grumbling.

Shine the Light

Why is it important not to grumble or dispute? "So that you will prove yourselves to be blameless and innocent, children of God above reproach in the midst of a crooked and perverse generation, among whom you appear as lights in the world" (**v 15**). This introduces the purpose or explanation of why grumbling and disputing must be abandoned—it is so that the light of Christ might shine through believers.

The word "blameless" (*ameptos*) means deserving no censure; being free from fault. It does not mean sinless, but being without obvious moral defect or blatant ethical blemish. Sinless perfection in this life is impossible, but to be "blameless" is possible—and part of blameless living requires that we live without complaining and murmuring. Put another way, it should not be possible for the charge of grumbling and arguing to be justly leveled at us.

Paul charges the Philippians to prove by the manner of their lives that they are genuine "children of God." They must give convincing evidence that they have been birthed into the family of God. To live "above reproach" (*amometas*) carries the same idea of being blameless. It means to be without blemish or imperfection. The challenge in regard to this kind of holy living is that believers (then and now) find themselves "in the midst of a crooked and perverse generation." The fact is, every generation is characterized by this crookedness. "Crooked" (*skolios*) is a very strong word for Paul to choose—it means winding, curved, twisted; while "perverse" (*diastrepho*) means to be distorted or to be turned aside:

> "People who are crooked are 'morally warped.' They cannot be trusted. They have arrived at this terrible condition by having turned and twisted themselves in different directions, but always away from the straight path pointed out by the law of God."
>
> (Hendriksen, *Philippians*, page 124)

So Paul's words here instruct believers to prove themselves to be different from the crooked and perverse generation in which they live.

Speak the Word

As believers live in a dark world, Paul says that they must be "holding fast the word of life" (**v 16**). "Holding fast" (*epecho*) more correctly carries the idea of "holding forth." The idea is not merely that we would have a tenacious grip on the gospel, but would also extend it to others. We must always be presenting the gospel of Jesus Christ to others with whom we have contact. In that sense, we must be holding forth the word. In fact, if we are holding fast to the gospel, we will hold forth the gospel—because its message of salvation contains its own imperative to proclaim that message. So Paul refers to the message as "the word of life," meaning it both possesses and gives life. This word alone is "living and active" (Hebrews 4:12) and imparts spiritual life.

> If we are holding fast to the gospel, we will hold forth the gospel.

Here is the necessity of speaking the word of life in their witnessing. The word must be more than the way in which Christians live their lives. This only provides the platform by which they are able to testify with their mouths. No one was ever saved simply because they did all things without grumbling or disputing. No one could be converted without the word of God being brought to them. "Faith comes from hearing, and hearing by the word of Christ" (Romans 10:17). In their witness to the world, the Philippian Christians must be "holding fast the word of life." As MacArthur puts it:

> "Just as right doctrine without right character is hypocritical and ineffective, so also is right living ineffective if believers are not proclaiming gospel truth." (*The MacArthur New Testament Commentary on Philippians,* page 185)

The Philippians must hold fast the word "so that in the day of Christ I will have reason to glory because I did not run in vain nor toil in vain" (Philippians **2:16**). Paul knows he will have invested his life well if those he has ministered to continue to be faithful witnesses of the word. "The day of Christ" refers to the time of Christ's return. They must keep witnessing until all the elect are saved. They must continue spreading the word as long as they are on this earth. If they do, that day will be all the more glorious for Paul.

On that last day, God will review every minister's work. He will reward them according to their faithfulness. Paul is saying to the Philippians, *As you lead your spiritual lives, if you are grumbling and complaining, I have run my race with you in vain.* His ministry with them will have been of little effect. His ministry in the word with them will not have been received as it should have been. They should do all things without grumbling and complaining as they hold fast the word and send it forth into the world, so that he will have reason to glory in the day of Christ.

"Glory" here does not refer to self-glorying. Rather, it means to rejoice. It is an intensive word that pictures rejoicing in the Lord. In this context, Paul is saying that as the Philippians work out their salvation, quit their grumbling and hold out the gospel, it will give him more cause to rejoice on that final day over what the Lord has done in them and how he used Paul in those purposes. This is how invested he is in his ministry and in those in his care. He cares more for their salvation and sanctification than his own freedom, or reputation, or wealth, because he knows that it is they who will be his joy in eternity: "For who is our hope or joy or crown of exultation? Is it not even you, in the presence of our Lord Jesus at His coming? For you are our glory and joy" (1 Thessalonians 2:19-20). We would do well, like Paul, to bear in mind what it is that will matter into eternity, and allow that to dictate our priorities and drive our emotions in this life.

Serve the Church

Paul continues, "But even if I am being poured out as a drink offering upon the sacrifice and service of your faith, I rejoice and share my joy with you all" (Philippians **2:17**). A drink offering was a God-ordained sacrifice that was poured on top of an animal sacrifice (Exodus 29:38-41). Wine was poured either in front of or upon the burning animal. As the wine vaporized, the steam rose upward. This symbolized the rising of the sacrificial offering to God. So, Paul's life is being poured out upon the lives of the Philippians. Their hearts and souls are being mixed together.

As we have seen, Paul first ministered to the Philippians when he came to Philippi on his second missionary journey (Acts 16:12-40). He spoke the word, led people to faith in Christ, was arrested, beaten, and thrown into prison. A church was planted. Now, even while Paul is in prison in Rome he is offering prayer with joy for them. In **reciprocal** fashion, the Philippian church has taken up a collection and given it to Epaphroditus to bring to Paul in order to pay for his expenses. They are pouring their resources into Paul, and Paul is pouring his prayers into them.

This partnership is a joyful fellowship: "I rejoice and share my joy with you all" (Philippians **2:17**). Paul is so full of joy that he shares his joy with them. Even though separated by these many miles, his joy is contagious. Few gifts could be more valuable to share with another person than one's joy. This is precisely what Paul does. No one can share what they do not possess; yet Paul seeks to share the joy he has in Christ with his beloved friends in Philippi.

Share Your Joy

Paul adds, "You too, I urge you, rejoice in the same way and share your joy with me" (**v 18**). In other words, they should share their joy with him just like his sharing of his joy with them. What was true of Paul was to be true of them.

Few commands could be more practical for our Christian lives. Even if you cannot rejoice in your circumstances, you can rejoice in the Lord. You can rejoice in God's holy character. You can rejoice in God's limitless goodness. You can rejoice in God's amazing grace. You can rejoice in God's perfect timing. You can rejoice in God's abundant supply. You can rejoice in God's all-sufficient provision. You can do all this even if you are sitting in prison, facing trial and execution. You can know joy even when your circumstances are not joyful. That is a precious gift.

Then Paul adds, "… and share your joy with me." Paul is a mere man like anyone else, subject to the temptations and discouragements of life. It is easier for Paul to preach this truth than to live it. It is hard for any preacher to live up to what he expounds. Paul needs other believers to come around him and share their joy with him. He needs other believers to come around him and minister to him. The same is true with joy. If Paul needed others to share their joy with him, how much more do you and I need others to share their joy with us.

> You can be, and should be, a channel for joy to flow to others.

This should cause us to think deeply about how we interact with one another. It should cause us to pause and consider how we can be a medium of joy from the Lord to others. You can be, and should be, a channel for joy to flow through your life to other believers. Do we share joy in the Lord with others, particularly when we or they are living through trying circumstances? Do we allow others to share Christian joy with us, particularly when we are in those trials?

Do you need more joy? How can you have more joy? All joy is in the Lord. Read his word. Be in prayer. Have fellowship with other believers. Be regularly in church. Magnify God's name in worship. Focus on the Lord. Trust the Lord. That is where true joy begins, and this joy will never end.

Questions for reflection

1. When are you most likely to grumble? What would it sound like to praise God in those moments instead?

2. How will the things that matter eternally shape your priorities today?

3. With whom could you share Christian joy today? Do you allow others to share it with you, even when you are facing difficult circumstances?

8. CASE STUDIES IN HUMILITY

What does Christian humility look like in real life?

That is the question posed throughout Philippians 2. After calling for humility (2:3-4), Paul gave the supreme example of lowliness of mind in the Lord Jesus Christ (2:5-11). That was and is the ultimate example of true humility. The second illustration was Paul himself, who poured himself out as a drink offering on behalf of the Philippians (v 17-18). Now we reach two more real-life examples: Paul's young son in the faith, Timothy (v 19-24), and Epaphroditus, a godly man who was the pastor of the church in Philippi (v 25-30). Let us learn from these two men what authentic humility looks like.

Humility Is Long-Lasting

The first of Timothy's virtues we learn about is what a long-lasting supporter he is to Paul: "I hope in the Lord Jesus to send Timothy to you shortly" (**v 19**). Paul is in prison in Rome, and Timothy is right there with him. This is not a popular time to be associated with the apostle. Timothy, nevertheless, is with him, even in these tough times. When others have left, Timothy has lasted. We, too, need to be long-lasting in our relationships with spiritual leaders. So many pay a great price to minister the gospel to us, and they need our continued support.

The apostle desires to send Timothy to the church in Philippi "so that I also may be encouraged when I learn of your condition." Paul will be encouraged when he receives a future report of their spiritual progress, just as they will be encouraged when they learn, Lord willing, of his release.

Humility Is Like-Minded

With Timothy in mind, Paul writes, "I have no one else of kindred spirit" (**v 20**). What an extraordinary statement for the apostle to make! As Paul traveled, he was surrounded by many co-workers. This team included such men as Barnabas, John Mark, Titus, and others who were a part of his ministry team. Timothy, though, stands out like a rare jewel to Paul. Timothy uniquely distinguishes himself as having the same mind as the apostle. "Kindred spirit" (*isupsuchos*) means "one-souled" or "equal-souled." Paul and Timothy are knit together into one soul—are one-minded and one-hearted; they are like-minded.

Who is like-minded with you? Such a person is a rare treasure for you. As Timothy with Paul, they will be with you in your times of greatest adversity. When others leave, they will remain. If you do not have such a kindred spirit in your life, pray that God will bring such a close brother or sister into your life. Everyone needs a companion like this. Even the apostle Paul had such a need. So do you and I.

Humility Is Large-Hearted

The second virtue that Paul commends in Timothy is his large-heartedness toward other people. Timothy is a man "who will genuinely be concerned for your welfare" (**v 20**). This young understudy is deeply concerned for the spiritual good of the Philippians. He does not have a superficial concern that gives an impressive appearance of caring, while lacking the reality. Rather, Paul says, Timothy is filled with a genuine, authentic concern for them.

"Concerned" carries a specific meaning, because it indicates having strong feelings for something or someone. It conveys deep emotions, and it can be used either negatively or positively. It is used in the negative sense later in this letter when Paul writes, "Be anxious for nothing" (4:6). "Anxious" is the very same word that is translated in **2:20** as "concerned." When someone is anxious, they are emotionally weighed down. In such a state, they are burdened and fretting. But here in **2:20**, the word is used in a positive way. Timothy feels deeply for the welfare of the Philippians, even burdened for them, and so he will serve them.

Not everyone, even in the church and even in leadership within the church, is like this. There are others Paul knows of who, "all seek after their own interests, not those of Christ" (**v 21**). Timothy is genuinely concerned for the welfare of the believers in Philippi, while these others are obsessed only with themselves. Paul is presumably referring to those jealous preachers in Rome who were slandering Paul (1:15, 17). These envious preachers are the epitome of self-absorption, the antithesis of any real humility.

Timothy is the exact opposite of these other preachers who are trying to pull themselves up by putting Paul down. He has a lowly spirit that allows him to be genuinely concerned for others. No wonder Timothy is so precious to Paul. Here we see the indispensable importance of being humble. If we are to be profitable servants, we must be self-denying, and not self-focused. If we are to be a useful instrument to the Lord, we must be large-hearted, just as Timothy was. Ask God to enlarge your heart for others. Ask for grace to care more for their welfare than for your comfort or reputation.

Humility Is Clearly Seen

Next, Paul points out to the Philippian church that when it comes to Timothy, they "know of his proven worth" (Philippians **2:22**). In the first century, this had the sense of being put through a special test and gaining a positive result. The word was used of testing a metal by putting it in a furnace in order to reveal if it was a genuine metal or an imitation. If it were a false alloy, the substance would dissolve. If for example it were true gold or silver, the precious metal would remain. Impurities would be smelted out, and the genuine metal would be all that was left. The true metal became purer as a result of going through the fire.

Paul uses this word elsewhere when he writes, "To this end ... I wrote, so that I might put you to the test, whether you are obedient in all things" (2 Corinthians 2:9). The church in Corinth was subjected to a test by Paul in order to determine whether or not they would obey the counsel of the Lord. Until these professing Christians were in the fire of adversity, there was no way to know whether or not they would obey and pass the test.

If Timothy had been untested in the ministry, he would have been a potential liability to Paul when tough times came. But Timothy is not a fledgling beginner. For ten years, Timothy has been battle-tested with Paul on the front lines of spiritual warfare (Acts 16:1 following). Though he is relatively young, only in his mid-thirties, he has been well educated in the school of hard ministry knocks and has passed with flying marks. Timothy has the spiritual scars to prove his advanced degree. He was with Paul when the gospel first came into Europe; he was there when the truth first came to Philippi; and he was there when the riot broke out, and they arrested Paul, dragging him into the prison. Timothy was there when it cost a high price to be on the ministry team.

> Obscurity is a gift in pursuing humility.

After those events, recorded in Acts 16, Timothy seems to have been left behind in Philippi to watch over this infant church as Paul continued down the road to the next stop. Timothy reappeared in Berea, and he joined Paul in Corinth (17:14-15; 18:5). From there, Timothy was sent back to Macedonia to minister (19:22). This was followed by five years largely of obscurity. However, that is what happens when you are a serving someone else. You are as often behind the scenes as you are on the platform. Obscurity is something of a gift in pursuing humility.

The point is that Timothy has been in many spiritual battles on many difficult battlefields. He has been through the fire in ministry. He is a proven, life-tested servant of the Lord.

If you are to be useful to the Lord, it will require that you be battle-tested. Realize that every trial that you undergo is intended to prepare you for future ministry. If you are presently in the fires of adversity in your service for the Lord—perhaps you are facing resistance or perse-cution in some way for your faith in Christ—know that God always has refining purposes in the midst of your difficulties. Your hardships are the training school for your ministry.

Humility Works Hard

A fourth quality of Timothy's proven character is seen in Philippians **2:22**. He labored. Ministry is hard work, and this is seen in the verb "served," which is actually better translated "slaved." It means to be directed and pushed by someone else in the work. Paul says that Tim-othy "served with me in the furtherance of the gospel." Timothy was at Paul's side on the front lines of the battle.

Timothy is a hard worker with a strong work ethic. He knows what it is to roll up his sleeves and expend energy. He is willing to perform menial tasks, putting in long hours, rising early and staying up late. He is ready to do whatever is required for the ministry to go forward. This sacrificial labor is what Paul commends Timothy for.

One example is seen in the assignment that he is about to be given. Paul says, "I hope ... to send Timothy to you shortly" (**v 19**). Then he writes, "I hope to send him immediately" (**v 23**). Paul says "send" twice—and it almost sounds like he is going to dispatch Timothy a short distance, like across town or around the block. But this journey that Timothy is about to embark upon is one of 800 miles, in a day when travel conditions were rigorous and tiring. And then once Timo-thy arrives there, he is to give the report and immediately turn around and retrace his steps for the entire 800 miles back to Paul. That is a total of 1600 miles of arduous travel; yet we see that Timothy is ready to do whatever it takes in the furtherance of the gospel. He is willing to pay whatever price to extend the kingdom of God.

From this, we can derive an important principle of all Christian ministry: ministry that costs nothing accomplishes nothing. There is a price for each one of us to pay in order that the word of God moves forward. What is the cost factor for you in the expanding work of the gospel? In what areas of your life do you need to step forward for the furtherance of the gospel, aware of the costs but committed to the task?

Humility Is Loyal

Here is a fifth and final hallmark of Timothy, which made him so valuable to Paul. Timothy is "like a child serving his father" (**v 22**). In their relationship, Timothy assumes the role of a child, and Paul that of spiritual father. Elsewhere, Paul calls Timothy, "my true child in the faith" (1 Timothy 1:2), "my beloved son" (2 Timothy 1:2), and "my son" (2 Timothy 2:1). He is obviously not referring to him as a biological son, but to his being a spiritual son in the faith. Paul was used by God in Timothy's conversion, and also in Timothy's spiritual growth. Paul was the chief instrument in the spiritual nurturing and equipping of Timothy for ministry. As a father figure, Paul gave wise counsel and oversight and direction to Timothy's life. In return, Timothy gives to Paul what a son gives to his father—respect, honor, obedience, loyalty, and allegiance:

> "Willingly, enthusiastically, the younger man had subjected himself, in filial attachment, to his spiritual father, for the latter's aim was also his own." (Hendriksen, *Philippians,* page 136)

"Therefore," Paul concludes, "I hope to send him immediately, as soon as I see how things go with me" (Philippians **2:23**). The word "therefore" is used here to indicate that this statement is a result of the special relationship between Paul and Timothy. Who else would Paul send, based upon what all that he had just said? To send Timothy would be to send the one who could represent Paul the best.

This requires on Timothy's part a large measure of flexibility with his schedule. It would necessitate a willingness to yield his desires and plans to those of Paul. It would require his adaptability, flexing with the priorities of Paul's ministry. Paul is confident that "I myself also will be coming shortly" (**v 24**). He does not know what will be the outcome of his court appearance, but he is remaining optimistic throughout this confinement, for in his heart he believes God has more work for him to do. Still, with no certainty of a release date, Paul will send the next best person to himself: his spiritual son, Timothy.

Humility and You

What evidence of humility do you see in your life that was present in Timothy? Maybe you are being tested in a difficult trial. If so, remember that God is always purposeful in his dealings in our lives. No trial need ever be wasted. God's purposes for us in our trials include conforming our lives into the image of Christ, and preparing us for future ministry. The school of discipleship always includes demanding assignments. For every Christian, trials are non-elective courses, and when God tests us, it is to prepare us for what lies ahead.

Next, ask yourself whether you are loyal to the spiritual leaders whom God has appointed over you in his church? Are you someone who is submissive and encouraging and who upholds those who serve you, rather than quickly becoming negative, critical and proud?

Finally, the Christian life is labor-intensive. Are you a diligent laborer in God's work? Is your shoulder to the plow? There is something for every one of us to do. No one just shows up. Everyone has a role and a job in the kingdom of God. It is a vineyard, and there are plows. And plowmen and plow-women are needed to do God's work. As we do that, we become like Timothy. And in that way, we become greatly valuable and increasingly useful to those who are like Paul—and, most importantly, to the cause of our Lord.

Questions for reflection

1. Why is humility not a highly-prized characteristic today, do you think?

2. What would it look like for you to adopt Timothy's approach to life and ministry in your own life and ministry?

3. "There is a price to pay in order that the word of God moves forward." What is that price for you?

PART TWO

The eighteenth-century missionary David Livingston launched the modern missions movement into the heart of Africa with a pioneering effort that would prepare the way for others who would follow. He once said, "I am willing to go anywhere as long as it is forward in the will of God." He lived out of his comfort zone, setting an example of sacrifice for the gospel. Such heroic fortitude is always necessary for the work of God to succeed, both in foreign lands and also increasingly in our own.

This is precisely the case with a man named Epaphroditus, who is highly commended by Paul for his tireless service for Christ. Here is another servant of Christ whom we need to know, because Paul regards him so highly.

Who Was Epaphroditus?

An initial introduction to Epaphroditus is in order before we consider him more carefully. He was closely connected with the church at Philippi. He was probably a spiritual leader in the church, serving in some capacity. He was sent by the church in Philippi to Paul, imprisoned in Rome, and he was to bring a financial gift from the church to Paul to help him with his expenses (4:18). Epaphroditus was also to minister to Paul by taking care of his personal needs (**2:25**). But while serving Paul, he became sick and then desperately ill, to the point of death. When news of this reached the church at Philippi, they understandably became deeply concerned. By his gracious providence, God brought Epaphroditus back from the doorstep of death to health and usefulness (**v 26-30**).

Once Epaphroditus had recovered, Paul sent him back to the church in Philippi along with his letter to them. Yet this was not his only purpose, as Dennis E. Johnson points out:

"Paul had another, not-so-ulterior motive in sending Epaphroditus home: the Philippians need another human role model to show them in a man they knew well, what it means in the nitty gritty of everyday life to share the mind-set of Christ so thoroughly that one is ready to serve to the point of death following the Savior's footsteps." (*Philippians,* page 180)

What were the distinguishing marks of this remarkable servant? And what can we learn for and apply to our own lives?

The first thing to note about Epaphroditus is that he was a genuine believer in Jesus Christ. There is a series of descriptions of this man that are packed into **verse 25**, listed in rapid-fire, staccato fashion: "my brother ... fellow worker ... fellow soldier ... messenger ... minister." There is not another verse in the Bible in which one person receives so many accolades as we see here. Paul is clearly absolutely determined that the Philippians hold Epaphroditus in high regard.

And the first description of Epaphroditus by Paul is that he is, "my brother." This man is a genuine brother in Christ. Further, Paul refers to Epaphroditus as not merely a brother, but as "my brother." This is a term of deep affection, indicating a close and cherished relationship. At root, Epaphroditus is a Christian. That is not all he is, but that is the start of all he is.

A Sacrificial Soldier

Second, Epaphroditus is also someone who is heavily engaged in the service of the gospel. He is identified as a "fellow worker" (**v 25**). Epaphroditus and Paul are shoulder to shoulder in the work of the Lord. They are plowing together in the same work of the Lord. There is no greater work that laboring with another believer than in difficult times, as this pair is doing here.

All believers should be like this because those who are in Christ are saved to serve. Every disciple has family responsibilities assigned to them by their Father. No saint has the luxury of being served, while not serving others. We must fulfill the task God has assigned us to do. As you consider your own life, how do you need to be more like

Epaphroditus, as a fellow worker with other believers? How are you investing your life for the gospel?

Third, Paul designates Epaphroditus as a "fellow soldier" (**v 25**). There is a logical progression that can be seen here. The more we work for the Lord, the more we will experience warfare for the Lord's cause. Epaphroditus is in the battle with Paul. His allegiance comes out most clearly in the midst of this imprisonment. In difficult times, it has become most apparent where his greatest loyalty lays. He must know that as he is leaving Philippi and traveling to Rome, he is advancing into the line of fire in spiritual warfare.

The same is true for every believer today. The more we serve God, the more we will find ourselves on the front lines of spiritual warfare. The devil is not going to oppose someone whose life is making little difference for the kingdom of God. It is the believer who is working for God, whose life is counting for time and eternity, and who is putting their nose to the grindstone who most often finds themselves in the midst of the spiritual battle. All servants should be soldiers. All workers must be warriors.

A Sent Servant

Fourth, Paul further refers to Epaphroditus as someone "who is also your messenger." He has carried an important message in war-like times. This word messenger (*apostolus*) in the Greek language is translated elsewhere as "apostle." It means one who is sent on an official mission. Epaphroditus was not an official apostle who saw the risen Christ (as the word is sometimes used in the New Testament), but he was one sent by the church in Philippi to minister to Paul.

Every Christian is sent by God with words of encouragement to others in need. Wherever the will of God takes us, whether across the ocean or across the street, we are to be taking a message of edification and affirmation to other believers. Further, we are to be messengers of the gospel to unbelievers in the world. We are to be speaking for the Lord wherever we go. Neither Epaphroditus nor we can be apostles in the same way as the twelve commissioned by Jesus himself were. But, in the way that Epaphroditus was, we are all apostles.

Next, Epaphroditus is described by Paul as a "minister to my need." This word for "minister" (*leitourgos*) is used only five times in the New Testament. It carries the idea of the priestly service of someone ministering in the temple by attending to holy things. It was also used of a servant of the king or a public servant of the state. This word indicates that what Epaphroditus is doing is a spiritual work; he is fulfilling a sacred calling. He is acting much as a priest would in going into the temple and offering a sacrifice. As Epaphroditus is serving Paul, he is, in reality, offering unto the Lord the sacrifice of his own life.

The 19th-century preacher Charles Spurgeon said, "If God has called you to be his servant, why stoop to be a king?" There is a world of needs around us, and we are called by God to be his servants upon the earth. What needs do you see before you, and how can you step in and be used by God to meet those needs?

The Emotions of the Humble

There is a further aspect about Epaphroditus that Paul highlights. This selfless man really is not concerned about himself, but about others. "He was longing for you all and was distressed because you had heard that he was sick" (**v 26**). The word "longing" (*epipotheo*) carries the meaning of an intense desire. Epaphroditus is possessed by deep, intense feelings for his fellow believers in the church at Philippi. Paul used the same word earlier to describe his love for Christ, when he wrote, "God is my witness, how I long for you all with the affection of Christ Jesus" (1:8). Epaphroditus is not a stoic worker merely going through the mechanical motions; instead he is one who feels deeply for other people, especially those in the family of God. He is genuinely concerned for them because they found out how sick he was; rather than be absorbed with self-pity, he is burdened that they are concerned for him.

Epaphroditus was not just sick, but was lying at the doorstep of death. But still his focus is not upon himself, but on the Philippians. He is more concerned about how they are reacting to his illness than he is concerned about his own health. He is "distressed." The idea is of being beside yourself. Why is Epaphroditus so disturbed? His distress is not caused by his own sickness, or his possibly looming death, or his continuing service of the imprisoned Paul. It is caused by the realization that the Philippians have the same concern for him that he carries for them.

> Ministry must be carried out not only with our hands, but with our heart.

What Epaphroditus felt for the Philippians we should feel for one another. Our ministry must be carried out not only with our hands, but with our heart. We must be emotionally connected with others in our service for the Lord. We must seek to feel with them, and feel for them.

Though Epaphroditus was "sick to the point of death … God had mercy on him" (**2:27**). God spared his life. Paul adds that this mercy was "also on me." This indicates how valuable Epaphroditus was to Paul and his ministry. God's mercy on Epaphroditus was, in turn, also his mercy on Paul. To spare the life of Epaphroditus was to show mercy to Paul, because the apostle had become so dependent upon Epaphroditus in his service to him. Again, we see the emotional connection between these two brothers and servants, between the prisoner and the invalid. What a gracious expression of God's goodness for Paul that he would spare Epaphroditus' life, "so that I would not have sorrow upon sorrow." Paul was not a man devoid of feelings. He was not a mechanical doctrine-fixated robot! Paul himself had deep affections for those with whom he served, and to whom he preached (see Romans 9:1-4). To have Epaphroditus taken from him would mean soul-wrenching sorrow.

A Willing Messenger

Moreover, Epaphroditus is a man willing to go wherever he is sent. Paul writes, "Therefore I have sent him all the more eagerly so that when you see him again you may rejoice" (Philippians **2:28**). The Philippians have not asked for Epaphroditus to return. They have sent him to Paul and presumably expect him to stay there until the apostle is either executed or released. But Epaphroditus is returning in what could well be perceived by the Philippian church as a premature manner. Consequently, Paul makes it clear to them that Epaphroditus is not coming back of his own determination. Instead it is Paul's decision to send him back.

Epaphroditus was sent by the Philippian church to Paul, and he willingly went. Now, Paul sends him back to the Philippian church, and, again, he is willing to go. In this we see that Epaphroditus is subservient to the needs of others. He is willing to go anywhere, do anything, and pay any price. Epaphroditus holds his life in an open hand and will do whatever would advance the cause of Christ. This requires great flexibility on his part, and means that he cannot set the agenda for his life.

It is this same kind of humility under the mighty hand of God that each one of us must exemplify. Every Christian must place their plans under the supreme authority of Jesus Christ. We serve at his discretion and must be willing to go wherever he would send us. Moreover, we must be willing to do whatever he requires. Is this where you life is? Are you willing to fulfill the will of God for your life wherever it would take you?

A Man to Honor

As a result of such a strong commendation, Paul writes, "Receive him then in the Lord with all joy" (**v 29**).

The apostle is concerned that when Epaphroditus returns to Philippi, he should not be critically interrogated regarding why he is back so early. He should not be cross-examined as one who has deserted his post. Instead, Paul exhorts the Philippians to "hold men like him in high regard." Such ministers of the Lord should be highly respected. "High regard" (*entimos*) means to give someone a high reputation. In other words, the Philippians should elevate their estimate of Epaphroditus due to the lofty reputation he has earned as a humble servant of Paul, and of Christ.

In Luke 14:7-11, Jesus told a parable about someone invited to a banquet dinner. Upon arrival, the guest should sit at the end of the table. Jesus explained that this person should wait to be asked to move up to the head of the table. If the guest advances to the head of the table, someone else more important is likely to come. After the seating, it will be embarrassing for the host to tap this person on the shoulder and direct him to the other end of the table, to make room for the one of higher regard. Instead, Jesus said, seek the lower place. Wait to be promoted, rather than aiming to promote yourself.

Then Jesus gave the application: "For everyone who exalts himself will be humbled, and he who humbles himself will be exalted" (Luke 14:11). Epaphroditus was a humble man, and an authentic servant, and Paul exhorts the Philippians to exalt him. Why? Because God exalts those who are humble and who serve.

After all, Paul reminds his readers, Epaphroditus has served to the point of death: "He came close to death for the work of Christ, risking his life to complete what was deficient in your service to me" (Philippians **2:30**). Calvin notes that...

"He would rather be negligent as to health than be deficient in duty."   (*The Epistles of Paul to the Galatians, Ephesians, Philippians and Colossians,* page 84)

Thus, this noble man should be highly regarded because he expended himself in the Lord's work with maximum sacrifice. By highly regarding Epaphroditus, the Philippians will be recognizing on earth the true greatness that is being recognized in heaven. They will be giving honor to whom honor is due. Men like Epaphroditus, sacrificing their lives in God's vineyard, are to be held in high regard in the church. He is an example of sacrificial servanthood to every Christian.

Through his word, God asks us to look at Epaphroditus and consider what it looks like to place the interests of others above your own. This choice servant of Christ is held before us as one whom we should emulate. Here is one after whom we should model our lives. What would it look like for your life to be given to God in humility in a manner worthy of the commendations given by Paul of Epaphroditus?

Questions for reflection

1. In what ways does Epaphroditus show us how to put others' interests above our own?

2. What would it look like for you to adopt Epaphroditus' approach to life and ministry in your own life and ministry?

3. If you had to explain to someone in a couple of sentences what humility is and how humble people live, how would you use Philippians 2 to answer them?

9. UNSPEAKABLE JOY

A Christian possesses joy that the world never knows.

Many assume that the opposite is true. They perceive the Christian life to be one of drudgery. They presume it is to live an antiquated life in which we deny ourselves every pleasure. But nothing could be further from the truth. The Christian life is filled with unspeakable joy that far surpasses anything that anyone in this world could ever know. In fact, knowing Jesus Christ is the only source of true and lasting joy that there is. The great Welsh preacher D. Martyn Lloyd-Jones once said:

"God's people are meant to be people who are always rejoicing in the Lord." (*The Assurance of Our Salvation,* page 13)

Joy is entirely different from happiness. Happiness comes from the Latin word *fortuna*, which became the English word "fortune." When my fortunes are good, then *fortuna*, or happiness, rises high. Conversely, when my fortunes are down, happiness drops through the floor. Happiness is entirely based upon the circumstances of life and can be experienced by both believers and unbelievers. Happiness is fleeting, temporary, and fragile. It is a moment-by-moment experience that can flee as quickly as it comes. As the word indicates, my happiness is based upon my happenstance. Joy is different, as MacArthur clarifies:

"The joy of which Paul writes is not the same as happiness (a word related to the term 'happenstance'), the feeling of exhilaration associated with favorable events. In fact, joy persists in the face of weakness, pain, suffering, even death."

(*The MacArthur New Testament Commentary on Philippians,* page 216)

True joy is not dependent upon circumstances. Neither does it come from the things of this world. Authentic joy comes from having a personal relationship with God through Jesus Christ. Real joy comes from knowing the Lord. This source of joy rises above our circumstances and cannot be drained by the surrounding situation. It is available in good times and difficult times, in prosperity and poverty. No matter what transpires in someone's life, they can know joy.

When times are good, it is not always easy to distinguish between the happy person and the joyful person. When times are hard—when disappointments and trials and sufferings come—then it is very easy to distinguish between them. The person who was happy becomes sad—even despairing or angry. The person who was joyful remains joyful. Happiness flees in the hard times; joy endures.

Happiness flees in the hard times; joy endures.

In the book of Philippians, the apostle Paul repeatedly addresses the subject of joy. Many argue that the overarching theme of this epistle is joy. As Paul writes about joy, he is describing something that is far greater than happiness. Joy is a divine gift that transcends all that this world has to offer. Joy is the supernatural excitement we experience in God himself; it involves gladness of heart in the things of God. It results from taking greatest pleasure in Christ and his kingdom above all other things. It is an exulting and an exhilaration in the soul, arising from a heart that is filled to overflowing with love for God and his Son, Jesus Christ.

This is the focus that Paul has in the first three verses of chapter 3. Here is an important part of the life of every Christian: the call of the apostle to all believers to rejoice in the Lord.

Joy Participants

Who can experience joy? The first three words of this section reveal the answer: "Finally, my brethren" (**v 1a**). "Finally" does not mean to indicate that Paul has come to the end of this letter. This is only the halfway mark in the book of Philippians! There will be another "finally" to come (4:8). This word (*toloipon*) could be translated "moreover," "furthermore," "so then," or "now then." This signals a new section in Paul's epistle in which he has much more to say. When he writes, "my brethren," this is a clear reference to the believers in Philippi. These "brethren" are those brothers and sisters in Christ who have been born again into the family of God. Together with Paul, they share God as their Father, and Jesus Christ as their Lord.

This joy is restricted to those who are the "brethren"—these are the same people referred to in 2:12. Such supernatural joy is experienced only by those who have had a supernatural birth. Non-Christians may know happiness, but they will never know this joy. The best they can hope for in this world is the emotion that is dependent upon their life's circumstances. A person who does not know the Lord cannot know this joy. It is reserved exclusively for believers in Christ.

Moreover, it is not an experience that belongs only to a few spiritual leaders. Neither does it belong only to those who have walked with the Lord for many years. On the contrary, joy is the hallmark of every member of the family of God, whether they are male or female, young or old.

This is the theory. In practice in our lives and feelings, though, are we always as joyful as we should be? Hopefully there is no doubt that we have a joy as believers that we would have if we were not believers. But as we look at our own lives, is the joy of the early church present in us? Do we know a contagious joy that overflows from our hearts? Are we growing to be more joyful in our walk with the Lord? Do not miss the challenge that we are *commanded* to rejoice. Do not miss the reasons we have for being able to rejoice—which Paul will move onto now. May we increase in our own experience of joy in the Lord, and may we learn from what else Paul has to say on this subject.

Joy Pursued

When Paul writes "rejoice" (**v 1**), he does not mean that the Philippians are to be frivolous or silly. Neither does he mean that they are not to fear God. Nor does this mean that they are to rejoice in sin. They cannot rejoice over that which breaks the heart of a holy God. Neither does this mean that they are never to cry or have sorrow. The Bible makes it clear elsewhere that there is a time to cry, while there is also a time to laugh (Ecclesiastes 3:4). Instead, Paul means that even in the most difficult moments of life, they can rejoice because they have joy in the Lord that transcends their circumstances.

The Philippians must not complain regarding their circumstances. Earlier, Paul wrote, "Do all things without grumbling or disputing" (Philippians 2:14). They certainly cannot have joy when they are complaining about people and circumstances, or have an argumentative spirit.

The Constant Command to Rejoice

"Rejoice" (**3:1**) is in the present tense. The means that the Philippian Christians, and we, are always to be rejoicing in the Lord. They were to rejoice not only on Sunday morning in their church gathering, but throughout the week in their homes and workplaces. They were to be always rejoicing in every circumstance of life. They should rejoice in good times, as well as bad times. They should be glad not only in prosperity, but in adversity. Rejoicing was to be their habitual emotion as Christians.

Moreover, this verb "rejoice" is in the active voice. This means Christians must take action to rejoice. We are to take charge in this matter. We have this obligation to direct our minds and hearts to rejoice in the Lord. We are the only ones who can fulfill this. God will not do this independently of our making this choice to rejoice in the Lord. When Paul states this in the active voice, this could be translated, *I command you to be always making every effort to be rejoicing in the Lord.*

In addition, "rejoice" is in the imperative mood. "Rejoice" is a command to be obeyed. It is an act of the will in choosing to obey God. To rejoice in the Lord is the responsibility of every Christian to choose to obey. Paul is commanding his readers to rejoice. They may not have felt like rejoicing, but that did not give them an excuse to mope around. That would be living in disobedience to this command. Believers are always to rejoice in the Lord. There are reasons why we become discouraged, some of them significant. But there are always greater reasons to rejoice. God does not command what he does not make possible.

Also, "rejoice" is a second person plural verb. This is to say, this command is directed to all the believers in Philippi. No matter where they find themselves in life, they must choose to rejoice.

Why should the Philippians pursue living a life of joy? Being joyful is necessary in order to live like Jesus Christ. The Lord Jesus is full of joy (John 15:11). The Father

> Jesus is most glorified when we are most excited about him.

has anointed him "with the oil of gladness above [His] companions" (Hebrews 1:9). Jesus is more joyful than any human. To be like Christ requires us to be full of joy and gladness. Moreover, rejoicing in the Lord honors him. Jesus is worthy of the excitement of our soul. He is most glorified when we are most excited and enthusiastic about him. If we struggle with rejoicing, we could do far worse than to turn to a Gospel, read it, enjoy the Lord and Savior we meet there, and ask him all the while to refresh our souls so that we would rejoice in all he is, and has done, and will do.

Questions for reflection

1. Why is joy better than happiness?

2. "Happiness flees in the hard times; joy endures." Do you find this distinction helpful? Have you experienced this in your own life?

3. "Jesus is worthy of the excitement of our soul." What is it about Jesus that particularly excites you today?

PART TWO

Joy Provided

What is the source of joy? It is defined in the next three words of Philippians **3:1**. The Philippians are to rejoice "in the Lord" (**v 1b**). The sphere in which joy is found is in a relationship with the Lord Jesus Christ. True joy is a gift from God that only he can give. The psalmist declared, "You have put gladness in my heart" (Psalm 4:7). And, "In Your presence is fullness of joy" (Psalm 16:11). This joy is produced by the Holy Spirit in the believer. Paul writes, "The kingdom of God is … joy in the Holy Spirit" (Romans 14:17). Again, "The fruit of the Spirit is … joy" (Galatians 5:22). There is not one drop of real joy to be experienced apart from him. All joy is in the Lord.

Paul writes, "Have this attitude in yourselves which was also in Christ Jesus" (Philippians 2:5) and looks ahead to the last day when "every tongue will confess that Jesus Christ is Lord, to the glory of God the Father" (2:11). This repeated emphasis upon Jesus as Lord makes clear who the Lord is when Paul says, "Rejoice in the Lord" (**3:1**)—the Lord refers to the person of Jesus Christ.

Joy Protected

There are many perils that threaten to steal the joy of Christians. Consequently, Paul says "To write the same things again is no trouble to me, and it is a safeguard for you" (**v 1c**). "The same things" could refer back to what Paul said to them when he was first with them in Philippi (Acts 16); or to what he wrote earlier in this letter; or to what immediately follows in Philippians 3. The reference is probably to the latter option. Paul has already mentioned "opponents" of the gospel (1:28) who are enemies of grace. These are the false teachers who have already infiltrated the church at Philippi. So now, as Johnson puts it:

> "From the bright motif of joy in the Lord, Paul transitions to a sobering subject." (*Philippians*, page 184)

Mentioning this warning about the false teachers "is a safeguard for you" (**3:1c**). A safeguard is a protection against falling and suffering great injury. Paul understands that he must address this danger of teachers who corrupt the word of God, or the Philippians will be headed for a certain fall into error and sin—and they will lose their joy. This stumbling block will trip them up and cause them to fall. Such a stumbling will bring inevitable pain to their lives.

False doctrine was threatening to disconnect the Philippian believers from their source of joy in Jesus Christ. False teaching always does. It may give happiness, but it steals joy. These false teachers had already begun spreading their perverting influence in the church at Philippi. Wrong teaching always leads to wrong thinking about God, which, in turn, always leads to wrong living.

Joy Polluted

Paul proceeds to describe these false teachers who threaten to steal the joy of the Philippians. They are the Judaizers. He writes, "Beware of the dogs, beware of the evil workers, beware of the false circumcision" (**v 2**).

"Note the threefold repetition, Beware… beware… beware… The three words are, as it were, blows of the gavel, signaling for attention, in order that the church of Philippi by giving heed may be safeguarded against spiritual and moral loss."

(Hendriksen, *Philippians,* page 149)

This Greek word for beware (*blepo*) means "to look at," either literally or figuratively. The reference here carries a metaphorical meaning. The Philippians must be on the lookout for these false teachers. They must be discerning and perceive who these Judaizers are. This is a strong word of warning that Paul issues. The idea is that they must be on the alert for these evil workers because of the danger they pose to the believers' souls.

These false teachers are first referred to as "dogs." This reference is not to a domesticated house pet, but to wild scavengers. These false teachers are like vicious, wild dogs that roam the streets in packs from one garbage dump to the next, devouring what has been thrown away. In this hunt, they attack innocent people and spread disease. These corrupters of truth feed on the trash of false doctrine. They spread the deadly disease of doctrinal error and moral decadence. They were marked by the uncleanness of their own immorality. They are vicious in character and attack the sheep. They are vile in their motives and filthy in their conduct.

Paul further refers to the false teachers as "evil workers." This speaks of their evil character, as well as their endless industry in spreading evil.

These false teachers are also the "false circumcision," which explains what they teach and impose upon others. The religious rite of male circumcision was taught in the Old Testament as a sign of God's covenant with the nation of Israel (Genesis 17). The death of Christ fulfilled the meaning of circumcision (Colossians 2:10-14). But these Judaizers were attempting to keep people under the old covenant by requiring their followers to be circumcised. Thus, Paul refers to them as the false circumcision.

These Judaizers were stealing the joy from God's people. They stripped the gladness out of their followers by putting them under the Old Testament Mosaic Law. Fulfilled in Christ, however, the act of circumcision was no longer binding upon the believers in Philippi. This requirement of circumcision and other such rules placed heavy demands upon the people.

Such false teachers are still with us today. They go by different names, but the false doctrine is essentially the same. They teach that human works must be added to faith alone in Christ alone in order to receive salvation. They teach that water baptism, whether of infants or of adults, is necessary for salvation. They teach that church membership is necessary for salvation. They teach that **last rites**, or the acquiring of **indulgences**, is necessary for salvation. Anyone who adds to salvation by grace alone, through faith alone, in Christ alone is a "dog."

Many today come from such religious backgrounds. Many have come from churches that teach baptismal regeneration or that salvation is in the church rather than in Christ, or earned by works rather than being given by grace. And many who have discovered the wonder of the gospel of Christ crucified for sins continue to carry some of that old baggage with them. Perhaps you do. Perhaps you wonder why your joy is elusive. Perhaps you wonder why you still feel guilty. Perhaps you wonder why you are still so crushed by your failures. Could it be because of the ongoing influence of that old manner of teaching that you once sat under and continue to carry around with you? If so, it is doing great harm to your spiritual life. It will rob you of the joy that is yours in Christ—joy that your eternity is secure, that his love for you is secure, that your salvation owes everything to him and nothing to you. You need to abandon those burdens. And, because the gospel is true, you can.

Joy Produced

But the call of Philippians is not simply to give up or resist the false teaching of "Judaizers." Positively, it is to experience and appreciate the gospel, that gospel which produces joy in Christ. So Paul now gives a description of the true believers who experience authentic joy in the Lord. "We are the true circumcision, who worship in the Spirit of God and glory in Christ Jesus and put no confidence in the flesh" (Philippians **3:3**). This is a black-and-white contrast with the false circumcision. This stands in stark distinction to "the dogs" of the previous verses.

Circumcision in the Old Testament was the cutting of the male foreskin as an outward sign of being set apart from the sinful world, in the service of the living God. It was a ritual that indicated what must happen to the heart. In itself, circumcision brought no redeeming value. It did not save, nor did it sanctify. It was a picture of what must take place in the heart. Circumcision stressed that there must be a cutting of the sinful heart that is hardened by sin. Such a stiffened heart can only be pierced by the Spirit. There is only one instrument sharp enough to plunge into and cut the foreskin of the heart—only one blade that can penetrate into the innermost recesses of the human soul: the sharp, two-edged sword of the word of God (Hebrews 4:12). When Paul writes, "We are the true circumcision," he means we are those who have had the word of God ministered by the Spirit to our hearts. We believers are those who have experienced internally what external circumcision was once the sign of.

In a second description of a true believer, Paul writes of those "who worship in the Spirit of God." Only the one who has been truly circumcised in the heart can worship God with their heart. The word "worship" (*latreuo*) means to "serve" or "minister." It refers to the performing of a religious service or homage. The idea is that this person ministers to God by actively, freely praising him. True worship must be generated by the Holy Spirit. It transcends all outward rituals such as circumcision, being prompted by the Spirit who indwells all believers. Such worship is to God the Father, through the Lord Jesus, by the Spirit. This kind of genuine worship is not and must never become restricted to Sunday morning in church. Worship produced by the Spirit is a lifestyle. It is the entire life of a believer given to God in spiritual service to him. Such worship is empowered by the Spirit of God. And it can never be stirred up by any outward ritual.

> Genuine worship is not and must never become restricted to Sunday morning in church.

These are the ones who "glory in Christ Jesus." Here is the worship that they give in the Spirit. They ascribe glory to Christ Jesus for who he is and what he has done, is doing, and will do. The word "glory" (*kauchaomai*) means to boast with great joy. True believers are those who are continually boasting in and about Jesus Christ and giving praise to him. We boast in what we find our confidence in. Any success that we have in our daily lives is attributed to the Lord. The one who is always glorying God in the Lord Jesus Christ and serving in the Spirit of God, seeking and finding security and satisfaction in him, is the one who has abundant joy.

> We boast in what we find our confidence in. Any success we have is attributed to the Lord.

Finally, the last description of the true believer is they are those who "put no confidence in the flesh" (Philippians **3:3**). "The flesh" refers to a person's own fallen ability independent of God. It refers to man's unredeemed humanness. There is an intended play on words here, where "flesh" is a reference to the practice of circumcision and the cutting away of the male flesh as well as merely human ability. Rather than putting confidence in the cutting of the flesh, the genuine believer puts confidence in the grace of God. But more than the mutilation of the male foreskin, Paul is referring to anything that someone does that is independent of trusting in God. It is anything that you and I might do apart from a reliance upon the power of the Holy Spirit, either to earn or keep salvation or blessing.

The Spirit of God and the sinful flesh of man can never work together at the same time; which is why Paul wrote to the Galatian church (who had fallen far further under the spell of Judaizing teachers and who were notably lacking in joy): "Walk by the Spirit, and you will not carry out the desire of the flesh" (Galatians 5:16). These two are mutually exclusive of each other. The Spirit and the flesh always work in opposition to each other and pull in opposite directions. The flesh is always self-reliant, while the Spirit creates Christ-reliance. The flesh always trusts in its performance; the Spirit gives confidence in Christ's performance.

Enjoy Your King

Each one of us must be joyful Christians. And each one of us can be joyful Christians, for we know the Lord. When we are glad in the Lord, we make the Christian life attractive to others. As the people around us see us walk in joy, it causes us to stand out in this world. Such joy is often used by God to draw others to faith in Christ. We truly enjoy the will of God and the task to which he has called us. When there is joy in our life, we emulate the Lord Jesus Christ, who had genuine joy even on the night before he was crucified (John 15:11).

How may we have this joy? There is no real, lasting joy outside the kingdom of God: zero, zip, none. It is only those who know the King and who are in the kingdom who know this joy.

So first, are you in his kingdom? And second, if you are, enjoy your King. Look to the Lord. Lean upon the Lord. Love the Lord. The key is the Lord. May each one of us learn truly and increasingly to rejoice in the glory and greatness of our God.

Questions for reflection

1. Identify some false teaching you have come across. How does that teaching steal joy?

2. What do you make of Paul's description of the false teachers as "dogs"? Why does Paul use such a strong word?

3. Think of the areas of your life you find hardest. What difference would it make to walk into them with your confidence in Christ, rather than in yourself?

10. THE GREAT CHANGE

Every believer has a testimony of how they came to faith in Jesus Christ. In these verses, Paul presents his to us. Any testimony of true faith in Christ has two parts. The first part is a description of life before conversion, which recounts how lost the believer once was in sin. The second part is then about coming to know Christ as Lord and Savior. This may include the time and the circumstances when they turned away from sin in repentance and committed themselves to Christ by faith. If a testimony were to be written as a two-volume work, volume one would be titled B.C., "Before Christ." Volume two would be A.D., "After Deliverance."

The circumstances surrounding our conversion differ from one Christian to the next. There is, however, one aspect that is exactly the same for every believer. It is that we received Jesus Christ in exactly the same way. Everyone is saved by grace alone, through faith alone, in Christ alone. And through these things, your life turns completely around, away from selfish pursuits and to following Jesus Christ. Your testimony is the particular, and unique, story of how this was made real in your life.

What is your testimony of faith in Christ? Can you recall your old life in sin? Can you remember the steps leading to your encounter with Christ? How has your life been changed since then?

In these verses, the apostle Paul recounts his testimony for the Philippians and for us. He wants everyone to see how his life was revolutionized by Jesus Christ. In no uncertain terms, he states how his life was radically transformed from the inside out. Before he met Christ, he was running fast in a wrong direction, a part of a dead religion. Then he was apprehended by Christ and immediately began running in the opposite direction. In these verses we hear the testimony of Paul in these two parts—B.C. and A.D. The B.C. part is deeply impressive and yet deeply lacking. The A.D. section is deeply challenging, and yet deeply liberating.

Before Conversion

Paul explains his life before his conversion in **verses 4-6**. Here Paul describes his old existence before he met Jesus Christ. "If anyone else has a mind to put confidence in the flesh, I far more" (**v 4**). What Paul means is, *If mere religious efforts could gain anyone acceptance with God, then I am at the head of that list.* Put another way, *If anyone could find salvation through his self-righteousness, that was me.* He lists all the things in which he once put his confidence. In **verses 5 and 6**, Paul notes seven different facts in which he once trusted, none of which could commend him before God.

■ *Impressive Beginning.* First, Paul explains that he had the right beginning. He was "circumcised the eighth day" (**v 5**). No Jew could have a more proper beginning than this. The Mosaic Law required that on the eighth day, a baby boy would be circumcised, which was the cutting of the male foreskin and the sign of the covenant. This ritual signified that there must come a time in which the heart of the individual must be circumcised as well. There must come the reality when that child is set apart by the Holy Spirit unto God. Circumcision was a religious ritual practiced by Israel with the significance that the heart must be cut by the word of God. But though Paul states that he, like all other Jews, had received circumcision, the fact remains that it cannot save the soul.

Perhaps you also had the right beginning. Maybe you were brought to church from the time you were born. Maybe you were sprinkled as an infant. Maybe you were dedicated to the Lord in a special church service. Whatever might have happened to you in your childhood, none of these things can give you a right standing before God.

- *Impressive Nationality.* Second, Paul had the right nationality. He was born "of the nation of Israel" (**v 5**). Israel was God's chosen nation, and they were the people who were privileged to hear the word of God preached to them. No other nation had such an advantage through access to the word of God. God gave his law, he sent his prophets, and he gave his commandments, all to the chosen nation of Israel. He made his covenant with them. So to be a member of Israel was to inherit a great privilege (see Romans 9:4-5). Likewise, there are people like this today who trust in being a citizen of a nation with a Christian heritage.

- *Impressive Lineage.* Third, Paul testifies that he was of the right lineage: he was "of the tribe of Benjamin" (Philippians **3:5**). Of the twelve tribes of Israel, Benjamin was one of the two elite tribes. They were one of the two tribes that remained loyal to King David's descendants when the kingdom divided; together, they formed the southern kingdom of Judah. In the land assigned to Benjamin the capital city, Jerusalem, was situated. So it was in the land assigned to Benjamin that the temple was built, and the sacrifices were made. Paul was not only an Israelite; he was of an impressive tribe. Many today presume that the spiritual lineage of their family tree will give them a right standing with God.

- *Impressive Upbringing.* Fourth, Paul adds that he was "a Hebrew of Hebrews" (**v 5**). That is to say, he was born of Hebrew (that is, Jewish) parents and was raised according to Hebrew tradition. He was reared in a Hebrew home and learned the Hebrew language. No one could be any more Hebrew than Paul was. He was a die-hard Hebrew. He was as religiously a Hebrew as anyone could possibly be. Maybe you can relate to this. Maybe you also had the right upbringing. Perhaps you were raised in a Christian home and attended a Christian school, and maybe you even learned the truths of the Bible as a young person. While these are all good things, none of them are able to save you.

■ *Impressive Standard.* Fifth, Paul had an impressive standard by which he lived. "As to the Law [he was] a Pharisee" (**v 5**). The Pharisees were those men most committed to the Old Testament Scriptures. They were Scripture believing, Scripture reading, Scripture studying, Scripture teaching, Scripture preaching people. They were fiercely devoted to studying the word of God. Moreover, they sought to keep it with all their might. So it was with Paul before his conversion; he was a walking, talking storehouse of Bible knowledge. Paul knew the Scriptures inside out. Maybe you are committed to the teaching of the Bible. Perhaps you know it well. Perhaps you teach it to others, or preach to your church. But even this, while noble and commendable, cannot save you.

■ *Impressive Sincerity.* Sixth, he had a notable right sincerity. Paul adds that he was, "as to zeal, a persecutor of the church" (**v 6**). Paul was not lukewarm about anything he did, and certainly not about religion. Paul was not apathetic, nor was he a "half in, half out" type of person. He was full of zeal and passion for holy things. He was filled with sincerity, so much so that not only did he love what he believed to be right, but he hated what he was convinced was wrong. From this character came his violent persecution against the church of the Lord Jesus Christ. He was a man who was filled with extreme enthusiasm for what he perceived to be the things of God. Compromise was alien to his nature, as much as Christ was alien to his view of God.

■ *Impressive Morality.* Seventh, Paul had a high standard of morality. "As to the righteousness which is in the Law, [I was] found blameless" (**v 6**). Had we been there, we would have stood back and looked at the life of before-conversion Paul, and concluded that here was a straight arrow if there ever was one. He sought to live by the standard of God's law. He was outwardly moral. He was extremely upright. And perhaps you are like this, too. You are well known as a good man or woman. You take following the Bible's commands very seriously. But this too will not save you.

Wrong Confidence

Paul appeared to have everything going for him before conversion:

"Humanly speaking he had acquired all the assets that anyone could imagine." (Boice, *Philippians*, page 169)

If anyone could have ever earned their way to heaven by their own religiosity, Saul of Tarsus would have been number one, and at the head of the line. This man who would become the apostle Paul had an impressive beginning, nationality, lineage, upbringing, standard, sincerity, and morality. Paul had everything except for one thing. He had everything… except Jesus Christ. And, as he was about to discover, if a person does not have Christ, they have nothing. He had everything except everything that he needed.

> Paul had everything except everything that he needed.

How does this first part of Paul's testimony compare to the first part of your testimony? Could it be that you once were lost in religion? Perhaps you were sincere about spiritual things, but sincerely wrong. Could it be that this describes where your life is at this moment? Maybe you are reading this and coming to the realization that you are a religious person but have never been personally converted to Jesus Christ. If so, it is important for you to know where you stand. A right diagnosis, it is said, is half the cure. But it is only half. You need to experience what now follows.

At Conversion

Next Paul writes "But" (**v 7**). That one word points back to the day when Paul came to know Jesus Christ in a personal, saving way:

"'But' marks Paul's experience on the road to Damascus when Paul first saw Jesus and learned what God's righteousness was. He thought before this that he had attained righteousness by keeping the law. But when he saw Christ he knew that all his righteousness was as filthy rags." (Boice, *Philippians,* page 170)

Once he met Christ, Paul was never the same again. So before we begin looking at the next verses, we need to look where "but" points us—to Acts 9, where Paul's actual conversion is found. Here is the greatest conversion ever recorded.

Right Encounter

"Now Saul, still breathing threats and murder against the disciples of the Lord…" (Acts 9:1). Here we see his zeal as a persecutor of the church. Paul was adamantly opposed to anything that did not adhere to his religious traditions in Judaism. He "went to the high priest, and asked for letters from him to the synagogues at Damascus, so that if he found any belonging to the Way, both men and women, he might bring them bound to Jerusalem" (v 1-2). The early Christians were referred to as those belonging to the Way, because they walked the narrow path headed to life. They lived according to the word of God in a dark and devilish generation—like stars shining in the dark. But Saul was in the darkness at this point—and so if he found any belonging to the Way, he was determined to "bring them bound to Jerusalem." He wanted to drag them back and have them stand trial, with the hope of putting them to death. The first Christian martyr, Stephen, had recently been stoned to death, with Saul standing by approvingly (Acts 7 – 8). Who was to know what Christian would be next? Who was to say how that circle of martyrs would expand?

"As he was traveling, it happened that he was approaching Damascus" (Acts 9:3), about 150 miles north of Jerusalem, when "suddenly a light from heaven flashed around him." This light was the *Shekinah* glory of God—the very presence of the living God—shining brighter than the sun in the sky.

Every conversion occurs suddenly. Every new birth occurs suddenly. It is not a process over a long period of time. There may be a process that leads up to conversion, but there is a moment, there is a time, when we cross the line; we step out of the world and step into the kingdom of heaven. This event, which we read of in Acts 9, is when Paul entered through the narrow gate leading to life.

Saul fell to the ground and heard a voice saying to him, "Saul, Saul." It was repeated with intensity: "Why are you persecuting Me?" (Acts 9:4). The glory of God reveals itself—or, we should say, himself—to be the One whose people Saul is persecuting: Jesus of Nazareth. To persecute the church is to persecute the head of the church, the Lord Jesus Christ. Jesus lives in the church as he indwells the true believers of the church. To come against the church of the Lord Jesus Christ is to come against Christ himself.

Right Confession

Paul's resistance against Jesus Christ was over. He cried out, "Who are You, Lord?" (v 5). If there was ever a time when the questioner answered his own question, this is it! "Who are you, Lord?" In that moment, Saul understood that he was face to face with the King of heaven, the Lord Jesus Christ. Instantly, he saw that he had been wrong all of his life. In that moment, he was apprehended by sovereign grace. Immediately, he confessed the lordship of Jesus Christ. In that split second, he became a believer in Christ. He laid down his life at the feet of the Lord Jesus Christ. He stepped across the line by faith and became a true follower and disciple. In that instant, Saul was converted by the grace of God. If there was ever a man who was not looking for Christ, it was Saul of Taurus. He was the epitome of what he himself would later write: "There is none who seeks for God" (Romans 3:11).

There is indeed "none who seeks for God"—but, in Jesus Christ, God is the Seeker. He came to seek and to save that which is lost (Luke 19:10). Christ is the great Initiator in our salvation. Our part in our conversion was running away from Christ. Whether we did so politely, religiously, or aggressively, we did so as fast as we could. Christ's part was to run after us, like the hound of heaven (to borrow a phrase from the poet Francis Thompson), until he tracked us down, apprehended us, and conquered our proud heart. Just as Christ knocked Saul off his high horse and brought him low, so it is in every conversion. It is Jesus Christ who is the One who has pursued us. He is the One who has subdued us that we might look up and say to him, "Lord." This must be our testimony, as well. We may never say, "I was looking for God, and I found him." We may only ever testify, "I was not looking for any God other than myself—and he found me." You did not work it out. Our seeking never does. He sought you out and he saved your soul, and this is the testimony we all share.

Questions for reflection

1. If you were in an elevator and had the opportunity to explain your own conversion, but had only a minute until you got out, what would you say?

2. Why does glossing over our sinful rebellion pre-conversion undermine our appreciation of what Christ did in our conversion?

3. When are zeal and an uncompromising nature strengths? When are they weaknesses?

PART TWO

Right Calculation

In Philippians **3:7-9**, Paul describes this divine encounter in the second part of his testimony. Here is the theological explanation of his conversion, expressed in accounting terms. In Paul's day, an accountant would have made a T-square. On the left side, he would list his assets, representing the profit side. On the right side, he would put liabilities, representing what he owed. Paul describes his conversion to Christ as an accountant would look at a profit-and-loss statement.

Paul begins, "But whatever things were gain to me..." (**v 7**). This is a reference to everything he has previously listed on the asset side of the ledger representing his life—everything in which he once trusted to commend himself to God (v 5-6). All of those things Paul listed before—self-effort and religion, upbringing and nationality—all of these were the things in which he earlier put his trust, and which he once thought would gain him acceptance with God. But they were not gain in the eyes of the Almighty.

And so, having encountered Jesus, "those things I have counted as loss" (**v 7**). This word "counted" is used three times in **verses 7-8**. Paul has added up the numbers and come up with a bottom-line calculation. Those things that he once counted as gain, he has come to see as loss. Everything in his life in which he once trusted to give him acceptance with God he has written off the asset column. He sees the bankruptcy of them. He has re-listed them on the liability side as a loss. In the moment when he met Christ, he rendered everything as loss:

"All of the cherished treasures in his gain column suddenly became deficits." (MacArthur, *The MacArthur New Testament Commentary on Philippians,* page 234)

Paul immediately saw them as that which would condemn him—not because they were negative in themselves, but because they were a bad debt when he arrogantly trusted them to secure him entrance to heaven. He saw that there was no profit in them whatsoever; there was only loss.

Have you made this transfer in your life? Did there come a time when you met Jesus Christ, and in meeting Christ you have come to see that everything that you once trusted in, everything you once hoped for, has just evaporated into thin air? It is worthless in commending you to God. Have you transferred it all over to the liability side and renounced it? And by faith, have you written "Christ Jesus my Lord" as the only entrance on the asset side of your ledger?

Right Change

When Paul met Jesus on the road to Damascus, everything immediately changed. "More than that, I count all things to be loss in view of the surpassing value of knowing Christ Jesus my Lord" (**v 8**). Again, "all things" refers to everything that Paul previously listed in **verses 5-6**—the bad debt in which he once trusted to give him a right standing before God. "All things" includes all of his education, learning, reputation, ministry, position, and prestige. These immediately became loss to Paul, in order that he could gain Christ.

To know Christ is to step out of religion (or irreligion) and step into a personal relationship with him as Lord. This means, as Hansen explains:

"the submission of every thought and every act (2 Corinthians 10:5-6) to Christ Jesus the Lord."

(*The Letter to the Philippians,* page 234)

To know Christ means far more than merely to know about him intellectually or historically. To know Christ means to know him experientially, intimately, and personally. It is not merely to know about him in your own mind. In this one moment, Paul came to know Christ on that Damascus road; he came to know him suddenly and he came to know him experientially.

It is from that point of conversion that for Christ's sake, Paul has "suffered the loss of all things, and count[s] them but rubbish so that I may gain Christ" (Philippians **3:8**). "Rubbish" (*skubala*) literally means garbage, waste, trash. It even meant excrement, manure, and dung. This man, once so highly-regarded within Israel and the Jewish religious hierarchies, is now in a prison cell due to their hatred of him and plots against him. He has suffered "loss" of reputation, family, nation, and security. But he counts those things as "rubbish"—trash that may be thrown off without a moment's thought or regret if it means he "may gain Christ." This is to say, the best that Paul once had to offer to God became as rubbish and trash in the moment he saw Christ. In that pivotal moment, Paul exercised faith in Jesus Christ, suddenly looking to Christ and trusting him for salvation. He counted everything as rubbish so that he would gain Christ as Lord.

The apostle realized that he could not have it both ways. He could not put his trust in all this religiosity and put his trust in Christ. It was all or nothing with Christ. It still is. It is renouncing the world and self in order to receive Christ. It is trusting nothing but Christ for salvation, and being willing to give everything up but Christ for the rest of life.

Sometimes people ask me, "Do you think that someone who is trusting in their baptism, or their church attendance or their church membership, or their good works, *and* Jesus Christ, will go to heaven?" The answer is a resounding *No*. You are not saved until you put both feet before the cross and come all the way to Christ. You have not entered the kingdom of God until you abandon any and all trust in any religious ritual and turn away from all your religiosity. You must acknowledge that all self-efforts are but dung. You have not come to Christ until you have said all else is nothing.

Right Confidence

Paul continues to talk about his re-ordered priorities after his conversion: now he longs to "be found in Him, not having a righteousness of my own derived from the Law" (**v 9**). He suddenly saw that he could never be found in Christ as a result of his own self-righteousness. He immediately grasped that he would never be right with God based upon his external morality. He realized he could never be accepted before God through religious ritual and ceremony. He could never be redeemed through his own good works. Paul is definitive about this, and for good reason.

Instead, here is how Paul came to know salvation—the only way anyone can—"through faith in Christ" (**v 9**). Salvation, or conversion, is by faith alone, in Christ alone. Period. End paragraph. Good works flow from faith, but they do not produce it and can never be a substitute for it. The great evangelist George Whitefield put it very well:

> "We are justified by faith alone ... good works have their proper place: they justify our faith, though not our persons."
>
> (*Sermons of George Whitefield,* 24).

Faith is turning to embrace the Lord Jesus Christ. It is acknowledging my own sinfulness, and it is acknowledging that my own righteousness will not commend me to God in heaven. It is coming to the place where I know I must have Christ. It is seeing that Jesus is the only Savior. The sole object of faith, of trust and reliance, is Christ alone.

> No one else went to a cross. No one else bore the wrath of God. Who else would we want to place our faith in?

This faith, however, is not ignorant or blind, but buttressed by the historical facts of the gospel. Faith, then, is rational. No one else was born of a virgin. No one else kept the law perfectly on behalf of law-breakers. No one else went to a cross on behalf of guilty sinners. No one else became the bearer of the wrath of God for accursed sinners upon that cross. No one else took sins far away. No one else paid in full the redemption for sin. No one else bore the wrath of God through his sacrifice. No one else was raised from the dead so that we might be declared not guilty and adopted as God's children. Who else would we want to place our faith in?

Paul then outlines what we receive by faith in Christ: "the righteousness which comes from God on the basis of faith" (**v 9**). Righteousness is to have a right standing before God through being declared justified—not guilty—before him. It means to be declared righteous by God, and before God. It is to be declared right before the supreme court of heaven. It is to find acceptance with the Judge of heaven and earth. This righteousness "comes from God." It does not come from within a person. It is not a self-righteousness, but a Christ-righteousness. It is given by him, and not earned by us. It comes from God and is received on the basis of faith.

That is what happened in Paul's life on the road to Damascus. As he looks back twenty years later, he describes exactly what happened in that moment with precise theological clarity. He explains his own conversion. He acknowledges that when he met the risen Christ, all that he had once trusted in he realized to be but rubbish. All that Paul once valued he saw as loss. And what he had once seen as worthy only of rejection and persecution he turned to as great gain. By faith, he gained Christ, who alone gives righteousness from God.

What Is Your Testimony?

Have you come to know Jesus Christ? Can you recall what your life was like before Christ? Do you remember how lost and empty you were? Can you recall when Christ made himself known to you by his gospel? Can you recall how he was suddenly everything?

Everything that you had once trusted in to give you acceptance with God you considered to be as rubbish. You transferred all your self-efforts and self-righteousness to the liability column. In the moment when you met Jesus Christ, you declared spiritual bankruptcy. Even your goodness was worthless. By faith, you made this one journal entry to the profit side of the ledger of your life: Jesus Christ. By faith in Christ alone, you found a righteousness from God apart from any good works on your part. This is Paul's testimony. Is it yours? And with whom will you share it?

Questions for reflection

1. Other than Christ, what would you be most likely to trust in for acceptance before God? Why?

2. "Good works ... justify our faith, though not our persons" (Whitefield). How is this a helpful distinction? What errors does it guard against?

3. Can you explain what it means to receive Christ's righteousness without using the word "righteousness" (or any other words a non-believer would likely not be familiar with)?

11. RUNNING HARD FOR HOME

A leading seminary recently surveyed its graduates to discover where it might better address any deficiencies in its program. The questionnaire asked its **alumni** to identify the one area in which they wish they had received better instruction. After three or four years of intense study in the original languages, systematic theology, Bible exposition, church history and much more, where did they feel most unprepared?

The result of the survey among these seminary graduates now in the pastorate was surprising, perhaps even shocking. The most repeated answer was: *How do I live the Christian life?*

This reveals that no matter how much of the Bible a Christian has been taught, we all wrestle with how we put what we know into practice. It does not matter whether someone is a brand new Christian or has a seminary degree, whether he sits on the back pew or whether he stands in the pulpit; all of us struggle to implement biblical truth in our daily lives. No one is exempt from this challenge.

Knowing how to become a Christian is relatively simple. The gospel declares that lost sinners are saved by grace alone, through faith alone, in Christ alone. The simplicity of the message of the cross is a reflection of the infinite genius of God. However, once someone is saved, the issue of how to live the Christian life is not so simple! Growing in the grace and knowledge of Jesus Christ involves many different factors. It demands that we deny ourselves daily, take up our cross, and follow Christ. It necessitates that we confess our sin and repent of it. It requires coming to the Lord's Table and remembering his death. It means walking in personal fellowship with Christ and with other believers. It demands that we are engaged in personal ministry, seeking to share the gospel with non-Christians, and actively living in the light of Christ's return. It takes putting on the full armor of God and resisting Satan's temptations. All this and much more is required in living a life fully devoted to Christ.

Unlike conversion, which is an immediate transaction from death to life, sanctification—growing in holiness—is a lifelong process. No one passage in Scripture contains the whole of what is required for right Christian living. The full counsel of God is needed to make known the whole truth of sanctification. We must obey all the commands, heed all the warnings, and apply all the wisdom in all of Scripture. Amid the many passages in the Bible that address Christian living, this next section of Philippians is rather obscure, and yet supplies helpful insight. In these verses, there are six aspects of right Christian living that Paul addresses. Here is how we are to live in order to honor the Lord Jesus Christ, and few texts could be more practical and relevant for our spiritual lives.

A New Priority

Having recounted how he had been converted on the Damascus road, Paul continues by describing his new life after his conversion. In **verses 10-14**, there are four distinguishing marks of his new life in Christ.

First, having been converted, Paul suddenly had a new priority in life. From then, the purpose of his life was "that I may know Him" (**v 10**). This knowledge of Christ became the chief pursuit in his life. We saw earlier that he came to know Christ at the time of conversion (v 8). If he already knows Christ, why does he want to know him who he already knows? The answer is that he wants to know Christ more deeply, and have a more intimate relationship with him. He wants to learn more of his teaching and draw closer to his heart. He wants to enter into a closer, experiential fellowship, a more intimate communion. As Boice summarizes:

"Paul wanted to know Jesus in the truest biblical sense—personally and experientially. And he wanted this to affect his day-to-day living." (Boice, *Philippians,* page 185)

Paul has written, "For to me, to live is Christ" (1:21). The whole life, the highest aim and the greatest priority of the apostle, and for us today as believers, is knowing Christ.

A New Power

Second, Paul also gained a new power for his life: "the power of His resurrection" (**3:10**). Paul wants to experience more of the power of Christ in his life. He does not want to live a mundane Christian life that could be easily explained by his own natural abilities. Instead, he wants to be a powerhouse for Christ, to exert a spiritual influence upon the world and to see transformation in others. But for this to happen, he needs to know the resurrection power of Christ surging through his soul. He longs for the very power that raised Christ from the dead to be more operative in his life. Paul needs this power to live a godly life, resist temptation, and meet every challenge within the will of God. The same power that raised Christ from the dead is what Paul wants in his life, to experience at work in his life.

A New Persecution

With Paul's new faith in Christ came a new persecution. So Paul adds that he is growing to know "the fellowship of His sufferings, being conformed to His death" (**v 10**). Paul understands that the more he grows to know Christ and to make him known, the more he is being called upon to suffer for him. Paul understands that "it has been granted ... to suffer for His sake" (1:29), because "all who desire to live godly in Christ Jesus will be persecuted" (2 Timothy 3:12).

And so, as he wrote to the church in Colossae, "I rejoice in my sufferings for your sake, and in my flesh I do my share on behalf of His body, which is the church, in filling up what is lacking in Christ's afflictions" (Colossians 1:24).

This was exactly as Jesus said it would be: "Remember the word that I said to you, 'A slave is not greater than his master.' If they persecuted Me, they will also persecute you; if they kept My word, they will keep yours also" (John 15:20). As the great Reformer Martin Luther is said memorably to have put it:

"They gave our Master a crown of thorns. Why do we hope for a crown of roses?"

A New Prospect

Third, Paul looks to the future and affirms that a glorious prospect awaits him. Because of his deep partnership with Christ in the suffering of his death, he will also share in the resurrection of Christ at the end of the age. Paul states that he is in union with Christ "in order that I may attain to the resurrection from the dead (Philippians **3:11**). This statement asserts the certain guarantee of Paul's future resurrection. Jesus Christ is the first fruit of the resurrection and Paul, along with every believer in Him, will be part of the full harvest, raised to share in Christ's glory.

Jesus taught this truth: "I am the resurrection and the life; he who believes in Me will live even if he dies" (John 11:25). Christ promised his disciples, "Because I live, you will live also" (John 14:19). It is the resurrection of Jesus that gives us such a glorious prospect beyond the grave.

A New Pursuit

Finally, Paul states that this new relationship with Christ means a new pursuit after Christ: "Not that I have already obtained it or have already become perfect, but I press on so that I may lay hold of that for which also I was laid hold of by Christ Jesus" (Philippians **3:12**). Faith is always active and dynamic, always moving us out and forward. Paul is acknowledging that he has not come to a point in his spiritual life where he can say he has arrived. There is still much spiritual growth for him to realize in his Christian life.

The verb "press on" (*dioko*) means to run or flee, to catch a person or thing. It is a word used of a sprinter running a race. The idea is that he is running swiftly after something, like a runner pressing on to the finish line. Picture the runner widening his stride, pumping his arms, accelerating his legs and pushing out his chest for the finish line. This is Paul's all-out effort to pursue Christ. He understood that Christ Jesus had laid hold of him on the Damascus road, and that he must press forward and lay hold of Christ every day of his life.

Paul knows he has not yet "laid hold of it," and so he does "one thing": "forgetting what lies behind and reaching forward to what lies ahead" (**v 13**). Here is Paul's singular passion to know Christ. He is forgetting the past, with all its failures and defeats. With an all-absorbing effort, Paul is reaching forward to the finish. He will "press on toward the goal for the prize of the upward call of God in Christ Jesus" (**v 14**). This goal is the full knowledge of Christ and full likeness to him.

Paul understands he will never fully reach this goal in this lifetime. But nevertheless, he presses on towards this "prize." Hendriksen has a useful insight here:

> "When this perfection is called goal, it is viewed as the object of the human striving. When it is called prize, it is viewed as the gift of God's sovereign grace ... Though it is true that this believing and this striving are from start to finish completely dependent on God's grace, nevertheless it is we who must embrace Christ and salvation in him. It is we who must strive to enter in. God does not do this believing and striving for us!" (*Philippians*, page 175)

As with any race, the prize is received at the end of the race, not during it. When he crosses the finish line—the line between this life and heaven—is when he will be given the prize. When Paul receives this upward call, he will not be found shuffling down the track. Neither will he be sitting down. Rather, he will be sprinting at full speed to the finish tape. And until then, he wants to be as much like Christ as he possibly can be.

A New Mindset

As Paul begins a new section, he calls for the right attitude: "Let us therefore, as many as are perfect, have this attitude" (**v 15**). When the apostle writes "therefore," he is looking back to what he has written immediately before. Specifically, he has **verses 12-14** in mind, in which he described his own, aggressive effort in pursuing personal holiness. Paul is not allowing what is behind to excuse him from pressing forward. Instead, he is running hard each day after Christ-likeness, looking forward to the finish line of his "upward call" to heaven.

This must be the "attitude" (*phroneo*) of every Christian. "Attitude" means to exercise the mind, to direct your mind toward a particular thing. A Christian must direct their mind to pursuing holiness. This must be every believer's singular focus. This implies that the Philippians must have become complacent in their Christian life. They must have become lukewarm toward the Lord; they have cooled off in their relationship with Christ. So Paul exhorts the Philippians to have this proper mindset for living in this sinful world. They must exert maximum effort in applying themselves to the spiritual disciplines of the Christian life. Right thinking is foundational to right living. God always starts with renewing the mind before he revives the emotions and redirects the will.

Paul addresses this charge toward those who are "perfect" (*telios*). He is not talking about sinless perfection. That is impossible in this life. "Perfect" can also be rendered "mature," which is how it should be understood here. The apostle is addressing those in Philippi who are spiritually mature. Perhaps his words drip with sarcasm because some believers assumed that they had reached a level of sinless perfection. By contrast, Paul has made it clear that even he has not yet reached this unattainable goal (**v 13**)—and, by implication, neither have they. They must resume running the race with all their might by the strength God provides. The Christian who has this attitude is the Christian who will make real progress in godliness. If there is to be right Christian living, there must be this right attitude.

As Paul exhorts the Philippians, we too should understand that this must also be our attitude in Christian living. No matter how long you have been a Christian and no matter where you are in your Christian journey, you must be always pressing on for greater growth in Christ-likeness. None of us have arrived. There is still much maturing to take place in each believer.

A New Insight

Next, Paul adds, "if in anything you have a different attitude, God will reveal that also to you" (**v 15**). He is alluding to the fact that there has been wrong thinking about the need to press on. The apostle is confident that God will make this known to them. This "different attitude" refers to the apathetic attitude of some in the Philippian church. For whatever reason, these believers have stopped running the race of faith with wholehearted effort. They are no longer sprinting to the finish, but have adopted a spectator mentality. They are no longer pressing on as they once did, but have slowed down to a casual stroll. They have succumbed to a sluggish mentality in their Christian lives and have become slack in their pursuit of holiness. So Paul says that God will reveal this different attitude to them—he will highlight their passivity and re-ignite their spiritual fire for him. They need to be shown their need to push themselves harder in their quest for maturity.

> In the Christian life, there must be no room for passivity.

In any Christian life, there must be no room for passivity. Every Christian must "work out [their] salvation with fear and trembling" (2:12). We must work out what God has worked into them. We must expend every effort in this hot pursuit. We must commit ourselves to the spiritual disciplines that will promote our spiritual development. We must always be moving on, always reaching forward to the prize of Christ-likeness. If we are not, there needs to be a serious mid-course adjustment.

So, ask yourself, is God right now revealing in you an apathetic attitude toward your Christian life? Is it possible that you have become slack in your sanctification? Have you become undisciplined in your Bible-reading and study? Have you become careless in your prayer life? Have you become half-hearted in witnessing for Jesus Christ? Does there need to be an adjustment in your attitude? If God should reveal this to you, will you be quick to change—to speed up once more in your pursuit of the prize? Increasing Christ-likeness—until the day we cross the finish line into Christ's presence, is too great a prize to let slip. If you are slowing, strolling, or even sitting down in the middle of the track, stand up and start running.

Questions **for reflection**

1. If someone had asked you yesterday, "How do I live the Christian life?" what would you have said? What would you say now?

2. "They gave our Master a crown of thorns. Why do we hope for a crown of roses?" (Luther). Why is this perspective on our lives both challenging and liberating?

3. At what speed are you running toward the finish tape? Use the questions in the previous paragraph to identify what may slow you down, and how you might speed up?

PART TWO

A New Standard

The Christian life requires the exertion of continually running hard after godliness. Next, Paul explains, the Christian life must be lived in accordance to an established standard. "Let us keep living by that same standard to which we have attained" (**3:16**). This "same standard" is the unchanging word of God. Specifically, it refers to the sound teaching of Jesus Christ and the apostles. "Keep living" (*stoicheo*) means "to walk in line with." It is a military term that pictures soldiers marching in a row. The idea is to keep in step with what is required. The Philippian believers must march in formation with the word of God. They must stay in step with the same truths which Paul had earlier taught them.

Apparently, some of the Philippians are in danger of departing from this divine standard. Subtle forces have been brought to bear upon their lives that are threatening to pull them away from alignment with the word. This shift in their thinking will, Paul warns, produce an unworthy walk in Christian living. There is no need for them to look for any other way to live.

If they should hear any new teaching, it should be rejected. If it is new, it is not true. New teaching is simply old heresy. The word of God is the unchanging standard, the immutable plumbline, forever the same. The Scripture is never outdated and never expires. And it is more relevant than tomorrow's newspaper. When properly taught in the Christian faith, they and we must keep on living by that same standard.

This applies to every Christian today. We can be vulnerable to being lured by the latest trend in Christian thinking. Many times it is false teachers who are selling their baptized humanism. They threaten to pull us away onto other paths. Many lying voices compete for our attention. We must detect them and reject them. We must remain committed to the same standard of Scripture with which we began.

Scripture has never failed, and has never failed us. There is no need for us to look for any other way to live.

Finding Mentors

Any growth in godliness is enhanced when we are influenced by the right spiritual mentors. So Paul encourages his readers to "join in following my example, and observe those who walk according to the pattern you have in us" (**v 17**). He addresses them as "brethren" to help them hear this correction. He seeks to endear himself to them so that they will receive his instruction. They must have brothers and sisters in Christ who are modeling Christianity and are worthy of their emulation. Paul is not being arrogant when he tells them to follow his example, but rather, he is being practical:

> Scripture has never failed, and has never failed us.

"Although his example is admittedly imperfect, it is, nevertheless, tangible and accessible to the church he founded. So, he takes the role of a mentor." (Hansen, *The Letter to the Philippians*, page 261)

The Philippians should pattern their lives on Paul's only to the extent that he is following Christ (1 Corinthians 11:1). If Paul's life is not worthy of such modeling, he would be disqualified from spiritual leadership.

This is the principle of discipleship. Jesus said, "It is enough for the disciple that he become like his teacher" (Matthew 10:25). As the twelve were to follow the teaching and example of Christ, so the Philippians were to follow the same in Paul. During his first trip to Philippi, Paul became their teacher, and they his disciples. The Philippians need to keep this godly example of Paul constantly before them. Paul wrote the same elsewhere: "Therefore I exhort you be imitators of me ... Be imitators of me, just as I also am of Christ" (1 Corinthians 4:16; 11:1). This is a bold exhortation, but proper and helpful. The Philippian believers should pattern themselves after Paul, who lived before their watching eyes, because Paul is further on in his Christian life and maturity. He is the living example of the spiritual instruction he brought them.

Of course, Paul is 800 miles from them. They cannot see Paul with their physical eyes in order to imitate his example. But in their mind's eye, they can still see him. They can remember how Paul conducted himself while in their midst, they can reflect upon the spiritual priorities he set, they can recall how he maintained his strong testimony for Christ in their pagan city, and they can distinctly recollect how he remained a bold witness in the face of mounting danger. These followers of Christ can recollect how Paul pursued the narrow path of daily obedience, even while surrounded by many snares. Though removed by this great distance, he urges them to remember his personal example and, more importantly, follow it.

At the same time, Paul acknowledges that he should not be the only example they have. They need to have other mature believers around them whose lives they follow. They should "observe those who walk according to the pattern you have in us" (Philippians **3:17**). "Observe" (*skopeo*) means "to fix one's gaze upon" or "to take aim at." The Philippians need to focus their attention upon other godly examples in their flock who model authentic Christ-likeness, which would surely include the overseers and deacons in the church (1:1). They need to note the lives of these godly men and replicate the pattern they set—their "walk." Maturity occurs through imitating mature believers.

Every Christian today needs to have the same kinds of examples before them. Wise is the believer who has several such people in their life as mentors and leaders. Misguided is the believer who thinks they have no need of these types of influences. Having an array of advanced Christians modeling genuine spirituality will produce a much more balanced, healthy Christian life. Those who have no example wiser and godlier than themselves will aim at nothing and hit very little; and those with only one personal example will likely eventually adopt not only that person's strengths, but also their weaknesses.

Moreover, every Christian must be a positive example for other believers. Other people in the church are observing how we live our lives. They are watching our actions and reactions. They are listening to our words and observing how we treat others. This places a great responsibility upon us in how we conduct ourselves. Jesus issued this warning: "Whoever causes one of these little ones who believe in Me to stumble, it would be better for him to have a heavy millstone hung around his neck, and to be drowned in the depth of the sea" (Matthew 18:6). We must never cause other believers to stumble because of the way we live. Instead, we must always beckon other believers into greater joy, faith and Christ-likeness because of the way we live. Ask yourself: Who am I imitating? And could others imitate me?

Best Avoided

Just as we must find good examples to emulate, we must also realize that there are bad examples to avoid. Paul cautioned them, "For many walk, of whom I often told you, and now tell you even weeping, that they are enemies of the cross of Christ" (Philippians **3:18**). To whom is Paul referring? It is almost certainly the "Judaizers" at whom he took aim earlier in this chapter, who were bringing a negative influence upon the Philippians and who were to be avoided like the plague.

These false teachers have come into the church and are spreading their deadly poison. Paul does not hesitate to identify them as "enemies of the cross of Christ." They are rank unbelievers—those inside the visible church but outside the Christian faith. Calvin described them in this way:

"They pretended to be friends; they were, nevertheless, the worst enemies of the gospel."

(*The Epistles of Paul to the Galatians, Ephesians, Philippians and Colossians,* page 107)

When Paul says they are the cause of his "weeping," he is broken-hearted because of the devastation they are inflicting upon the church.

We can imagine Paul weeping over their lost condition and the eternal destruction they face (see, for instance, Romans 9:1-3). But here, he is mourning the spread of their lethal doctrine. Paul is lamenting their soul-damning heresies and the devastating influence they bring, and he cannot think of this precious church without weeping over the destructive effects this false teaching has.

With a rapid-fire series of descriptions of these spiritual enemies, Paul minces no words. He exposes them as people "whose end is destruction, whose god is their appetite, and whose glory is in their shame, who set their minds on earthly things" (Philippians **3:19**). Their "end" refers to their eternal destiny, which is "destruction," or eternal damnation. Their "god is their appetite." This refers not to their physical hunger, but, metaphorically, to their sensual lusts. They worship what feels right, or what feels good. Their own desires are elevated to the level of divine authority in their lives. These religious teachers have an unrestrained and insatiable appetite for the unlawful fleshly desires within them. Further, their "glory is in their shame." This describes their self-boasting in which they glory in themselves. They elevate themselves in their own eyes before others. This self-glory is disgraceful, and the polar opposite of true servant leaders. Their self-absorbed attitude is the antithesis of genuine humility, which Paul has gone to great lengths to describe.

Our generation is not so very different. Many leaders in ministry today act in the same self-promoting fashion, drawing attention to themselves as they indulge their own fleshly appetites. Those who preach a prosperity gospel of the "name it, claim it" mentality offer a "get-rich-quick scheme" under the supposed guise of Christianity. Such false teachers are egomaniacs, parading like peacocks, strutting their way to divine judgment. Unfortunately, there are gullible people everywhere who lack the discernment to avoid such teachers. These teachers set their minds on their own personal advancement, while luring others onto the road to destruction. It should be enough to make us weep, just as it was for Paul.

Citizens of a Higher Kingdom

As Paul concludes this section, he directs the attention of the Philippians upward to heaven in anticipation of the return of Jesus Christ. "Our citizenship is in heaven, from which also we eagerly wait for a Savior, the Lord Jesus Christ" (**v 20**). In the first century, "citizenship" referred to a colony of non-citizens living in a foreign land. Paul is reminding them that even though they live in the Roman colony of Philippi, their real citizenship is in another place. Their names are permanently recorded where the King of kings, Jesus Christ, is enthroned at the right hand of God. They are citizens of two distant cities:

> "To be a citizen of Philippi was to be a citizen of distant Rome, where Caesar ruled his far-flung empire, with all the attendant privileges and responsibilities. So also Jesus-followers in Philippi, whether their status in society was slave or citizen or something in between, were citizens of a distant cosmic capital, of heaven itself, where their Savior and Lord, Jesus Christ, infinitely mightier than Roman emperors, was ruling the universe."
>
> (Johnson, *Philippians,* page 236)

While they are still living in Philippi, Paul therefore reminds them that they must "eagerly wait" with great expectation for Jesus Christ to return from heaven. In that moment, he will appear and take them to their eternal home. Paul uses four names here to describe his Master, each with great significance. "Savior" means "the one who delivers from great dangers"; "Jesus" means "God saves"; "Christ" means "the Anointed one, the King"; "Lord" means "Ruler, Sovereign." By using these four names, Paul gives a more comprehensive and weighty sense of the One who is coming for them.

At his triumphant return, Christ "will transform the body of our humble state into conformity with the body of His glory" (**v 21**). This dramatic appearing will alter not only the souls and spirits of believers, but also our frail bodies. Right now, our bodies are in a "humble state," subject to the weaknesses, diseases, and death of this world. But when Jesus returns, our bodies will be made like his own resurrected, glorified body. We will have a heavenly body perfectly suited for our new environment. We will be enabled to worship and serve Christ throughout all eternity and never grow weary in our new eternal occupation in the country we call home. In that final state, our worship will be made perfect.

This radical makeover will occur "by the exertion of the power that He has even to subject all things to Himself" (**v 21**). By the supreme power of Jesus Christ, God will overrule the natural laws of sin and death that have inflicted destruction upon the human body. This One who is "the resurrection and the life" (John 11:25) will deliver not only our souls from danger, but also our bodies from decay, transforming them into their final state of glorification.

This is the eager anticipation that all of us can have and should have. Every Christian must be looking and longing for the return of Jesus Christ. We must not become so preoccupied with the concerns of this present world that we become distracted from the "blessed hope" (Titus 2:13) of his coming. In that decisive moment, everything will undergo a radical transformation. Our bodies will be glorified, our sinful nature will be eradicated, and our souls will be made into the full likeness of Christ. This future grace must occupy our minds and capture our hearts as we live in this present "humble state."

> Jesus will deliver not only our souls from danger, but also our bodies from decay.

We must never forget that each of us who name Jesus as King is a citizen of a higher kingdom. This world is not our home. But as we live out our days here on earth, we must maintain our greater allegiance to our Sovereign Lord, who is seated at the right hand of the Majesty on high. We must never cave in to the surrounding pressures to squeeze us into the mold of this rebellious world. Instead, we must set our minds on things above, not upon things below.

We are heading for the finish line. We are headed for home. That is where we belong, and we must run hard until our King returns, or until he calls us home.

Questions for reflection

1. "How do I live the Christian life?" How has the second part of this chapter added to your answer? Has it surprised you in any way?

2. Who is your mentor? Do you need humbly to ask an older Christian to serve you in this way? Or is there someone who you could, in your turn, seek to mentor?

3. How does considering your future life in Christ's kingdom after he returns encourage you to live as a citizen of that kingdom today?

12. CONFLICT MANAGEMENT

The most practical course I took while I was studying at seminary was named "Conflict Management." But I still began my first pastorate unprepared for what awaited me. Hidden from my initial sight, I stepped into a church that was full of conflict at every level. There was relational conflict, doctrinal strife, philosophical differences, leadership unrest, and financial pressures. For someone raised in a home without drama, this was a crash course in the difficulties of dealing with difficult people.

Nothing could be more relevant in many churches than the proper management of conflict. Since the dawn of human history, beginning with Cain and Abel (Genesis 4:1-16), there has been conflict between individuals. No church escapes this friction. Wherever there are people, there is the potential for conflict. Such turbulence can threaten the effectiveness of the church's ministries. Consequently, whenever conflict arises in the church, it must be properly addressed and rightly resolved.

The dictionary defines "conflict" as a serious disagreement, an argument, a long-lasting armed struggle, a lack of agreement. Synonyms for this word "conflict" are dispute, quarrel, squabble, dissension, clash, discord, friction, strife, hostility, disputation, contention, feud or schism. All of this and more describes what conflict is. It is sad to say, but true to report, that conflict is too often found in the church of Jesus Christ.

The church in Philippi was no different. As great as this church was, there nevertheless was strife. So the apostle Paul writes to the church in Philippi to address this problem. There were two women at the heart of this brewing storm. He calls them out by name; permanently recorded in the word of God. Their strife was creating a rift in the fellowship of the church; and it had reached a point where Paul felt he must address them publicly. As this letter was read to the entire church when it was delivered from Rome, there was no doubt in anyone's mind what the problem was in this church. It was these two women who could not get along.

Paul begins this small section with the word "therefore" (Philippians **4:1**). This serves as a bridge that connects two units of thought. It reaches back to what he previously wrote and brings it to a bottom-line conclusion. The previous chapter had a strong emphasis upon doctrine. All truth must be followed with a "therefore," because all truth has implications for daily life. This word, then, introduces to the Philippians the practical application of what Paul has been teaching. In his application, he addresses the Philippians in five distinct ways, using five words and phrases that come flowing out of his heart. He is careful to speak the truth in love.

A Compassion Expressed

The first words in which Paul addresses the Philippians are "my beloved" (**v 1**). No more tender word could be used to express his love for another than to refer to them as "beloved." This goes far beyond affirming his love for them. The personal pronoun "my" makes this personal and intimate. The Philippians were closely connected in the family of God.

"Beloved" is an adjective that amplifies the "brethren." The apostle seems to be adding one affectionate term upon another as he addresses them. He cherished the reality that they were brothers and sisters together in the same family of God. This term indicates a deep, abiding relationship that they enjoyed with one another. And it underlines the seriousness and tragedy of conflict within their fellowship.

Moreover, Paul is writing to those "whom I long to see." This verb, "long" (*epipothetos*), expresses a strong desire marked by intense affection. This is a rare word, and this instance is the only time it is used in the New Testament. He reserves this level of deep affection for this church in Philippi, which has gained such a special place in his heart. In addition, Paul identifies them as "my joy," the cause for great excitement in his heart. If you could pull back the veil over his heart and look into his soul, you would see exuberant joy abounding in his heart for them. As he reflects upon them, remembering their coming to faith in Christ and their strong stand for Christ in a pagan land, they bring him much joy.

Finally Paul writes that this church is his "crown." "Crown" refers to the victor's crown that was given to the athlete who won an event. The presiding judge would place a laurel wreath upon the victor's head. This "crown" represented that he had run the race and won. In this very tender way, Paul is saying that they will be the wreath on his head, the crown that will be given as the proof that he has run his race victoriously. As he thinks of them, he knows that his labor has not been in vain. They have received the word from Paul, and they are running their race. As a result, these Philippians believers are the crown upon his head.

Who is the crown upon your head? To whom have you passed on the word of God? A son or daughter? A person to whom you have witnessed for Christ? The members of your small-group Bible study? A colleague at work? Since they have received the gospel from you, do you see them as your crown? Can you give thanks for the joy which their faith has brought to your life?

A Charge Given

Paul now speaks directly to the Philippians. "In this way" (**v 1**) refers back to how he has previously spoken of himself in the preceding chapter. As he has stood firm for the gospel, so they too must "stand firm" (**v 1**). They should look to Paul as an example of being immoveable in the will of God. "Stand firm" (*steko*) is a military charge from a commanding officer to his soldiers, charging them to hold their position on the battlefield. Why is this so urgent? Because, as the British commentator Alec Motyer points out:

"They are in the midst of enemies, especially the 'enemies of the cross of Christ' (3:18). There is a real danger that they will be drawn away by their present threat and a consequent need for a resolute stand." (*The Message of Philippians,* page 199)

Paul is saying to the Philippians that they must understand they are in spiritual warfare and are positioned like soldiers on the frontline. They must hold their position in the midst of a godless culture. They must not compromise over the gospel. They must not collapse under the pressure of persecution. They must never retreat and yield the high ground of divine truth. They must not go **AWOL** and flee from the battlefield. They must stand firm in what they have been taught.

They must remain steadfast, Paul writes, "in the Lord" (**4:1**). This firm stance is not in their traditions or in the natural human's way of thinking, but rather they must hold their ground "in the Lord." This means in the truth and resources which God provides. If they are to stand firm, it cannot be in their own strength or wisdom. They can only stand firm as they are reliant upon the Lord. If they are to stand for the Lord, they must stand in the Lord.

In like manner, you and I must stand firm in the Lord as we face the many challenges that are before us. As Paul instructed the Philippians, so we also must hold our position where the Lord has placed us in this world, standing firm in our witness for Jesus Christ. We must be firmly rooted and grounded in the word of God, and dependent upon the power of the indwelling Spirit.

A Conflict Addressed

After expressing his love for them, Paul addresses the problem that was festering within this congregation. Putting his finger on the live nerve, he writes, "I urge Euodia and I urge Syntyche to live in harmony" with one another (**v 2**). Obviously, these two women were at odds with one

another. Christians are not immune from disagreement and disharmo-
ny, as Motyer writes:

"Relationships can become atrociously tangled, and Christian relationships are no exceptions."

(*The Message of Philippians,* page 203)

This squabble was serious enough that Paul incorporated it into this
small letter of only four chapters.

What do we know about Euodia and Syntyche? They were two
women who were members of the Philippian church. Apparently,
they were well-known members of this congregation, and fellow
workers with Paul in the gospel, as **verse 3** states. These were not
obscure members in the life of
this flock. These were frontline
warriors—two servants who had
put their shoulders to the plow in
the cause of the gospel. They had
been laboring side by side when
Paul was there, and were heavily
involved in the life of this church.
The problem was not that they
were not involved because they
worked hard in God's labors. The problem was that they were not
united, suffering a serious disagreement that was quite a clash. Even
worse, their breach was affecting the unity of the entire church. The
friction between these two was disrupting the spiritual life of those
around them to the point that this feud was fracturing the fellowship of the church.

> The problem was not that they were not involved but that they were not united.

Paul urged these two women to live in harmony because this was
the very thing they were not doing. This was not a small feud in
this church, but a major problem threatening its strength and witness. This conflict was not theological, but relational. The problem
was that these two women were in conflict with one another and
remained unreconciled.

Usually, there is a progression in how something like this escalates within a person's spirit. Paul outlines this elsewhere: "Let all bitterness and wrath and anger and clamor and slander [that is quite a list] be put away from you, along with all malice" (Ephesians 4:31). Things begin with "bitterness" and conclude with "malice." Paul has a logical sequence in mind. There is an unfolding from one error to the next, and then on to the next. Our initial heart problem begins with "bitterness," meaning a resentment or grudge. It starts out relatively small, but as irritability begins to fester, a sour spirit develops as an attitude problem.

If unaddressed, our bitterness progresses to "wrath," describing wild rage that escalates on the inside. It builds and builds until it leads to you losing your temper. Something is said that punches a hot button. When bitterness has built up, a single spark will cause an explosion. Suddenly, you fly off the handle and say something in a moment of rage. This then leads to "anger," which is an internal smoldering, a deeper feeling of animosity. That moment of wrath does not go away, but settles in and brews into ongoing anger. Wrath erupts in a moment, but anger is long lasting.

> When bitterness has built up, a single spark will cause an explosion.

From there, anger builds to "clamoring." This word speaks of a public outburst in front of other people. There is no restraint now, but an outward loss of self-control. We begin to speak without any fear of reprisals. This, in turn, leads to "slander," which is a character assassination of someone. Finally, there is "malice," which is the proliferation of evil. Evil motives are assigned, and evil thoughts are carried out in evil actions. This entire parade started out as a small measure of resentment or a minor grudge; it ends in malicious evil.

This undoubtedly was the problem with these two women in the church at Philippi. It was not a doctrinal problem as this was a well-taught church. Their problem was strictly a relational one.

This problem must never be allowed to fester in any of our relationships within the body of Christ. Perhaps you are currently involved in a conflict with another family or church member. If this is the case, I urge you to take decisive steps to be a peacemaker. Initiate ways to work through the awkwardness in the relationship. Build a bridge to the others who are involved instead of remaining withdrawn. This will honor God and exemplify the gospel.

Questions for reflection

1. Why is conflict often so attractive to us, even as it wearies us? Why is conflict so hard to resolve?

2. How does positively and consciously standing firm in the Lord pull us out of conflict with each other?

3. Do you need to take any decisive steps to make peace with a fellow believer? How will you do that today?

PART TWO

Paul's Plea

Euodia and Syntyche are fellow Christians, but they are hardly in fellowship with each other. We can infer that the whole church is affected, since Paul chooses to address the problem publicly. He urges them "to live in harmony in the Lord" (Philippians **4:2**). In this verse, Paul twice uses the verb "urge," which doubly underscores the strength of his pleading. It would have been one thing if Paul had written, "I urge Euodia and Syntyche," as if speaking to them collectively. But he singles out each of them individually, urging each woman separately. Regardless of how the other one will respond, Paul urges each one of them, personally and directly, to act. "Urge" (*parakaleo*) carries the idea of a strong pleading and fervent imploring. Paul is exhorting them with a warmhearted appeal. This is not a plea that they can afford to neglect.

Specifically, Paul urges them "to live in harmony." This is actually just one word in the original Greek language (*phroneo*) and means, literally, "to exercise the mind." The idea is to direct their minds to be together in addressing this problem. Paul has used this word several times already in this letter: "Make my joy complete by being of the same mind" (2:2). "Have this attitude in yourselves" (2:5). "Let us therefore, as many as are perfect, have this attitude" (3:15). Paul is saying that these women must have the same mind in this matter. They must get in the same boat and start rowing in the same direction. They must adopt the same mindset, which will bring reconciliation and restoration in their relationship.

These two women, Paul adds, must live harmoniously "in the Lord" (**4:2**). This is the sphere in which they were to find their harmony. When he says, "in the Lord," he means that the Lord must be their common ground. Each must be in submission to the Lord. If they will first be in alliance with the Lord, then they will be in harmony with each other. The Lord is the common denominator, who will establish true unity between these two women. In other words, they both must first be right with God. Just as Paul, in the first part of this letter, established the basis for salvation, so too must these women build upon their common salvation "in the Lord" to resolve this dispute.

As they yield to the Lord, he will give them patience with and forgiveness for the other person. The Lord will give them humility of mind to bury the hatchet. But they must confess their sin, and each be a peacemaker toward the other. Only in the Lord will this be resolved. If there is not a true oneness in the Lord, this will not work.

This applies to each one of us today. This is an appeal for every believer to live in harmony with others in the church. Our conflicts are not spiritually neutral—they undermine the church, and they display a lack of submission to the Lord, by at least one and usually two parties. And in resolving conflicts, we are never to be passive, waiting for the other to apologize or change. Through Paul, the Lord urges all who call upon his name to seek reconciliation with each other. This is rarely easy, but it is always right. It is the Christian way.

Help Needed

Paul realizes it will be difficult for these two ladies to work this out. The wounds appear deep and the hurt has presumably been there for some time (otherwise Paul would not have heard about it). Consequently, he appeals to another member of the church in Philippi to step in and act as a peacemaker. A reconciler is needed who will bring these two women together.

Notice that he says, "Indeed, true companion, I ask you also to help…" (**v 3**). "Indeed" introduces the strong affirmation that follows. What he is about to say must be brought to pass. This peacemaker is a "true companion," meaning "genuine," "legitimate." There are other so-called companions who are not having a positive role in the fellowship. But there are true companions who are true friends and true peacemakers.

When Paul says "companion," it is unclear whether it is a description of this person, or this person's actual name. Many translate "companion" as a description of the individual but the stronger evidence is that this is their name. In **verse 2**, there are two names, Euodia and Syntyche. In **verse 3**, the name Clement appears. Placed in the middle between Euodia and Syntyche and Clement is this person, whose name is Syzygos. He was probably one of the overseers or elders mentioned in Philippians 1:1, since one of the roles of leaders in the church is to shepherd the flock when disputes arise that are that personally or corporately harmful. So this spiritual leader was being asked to step in and resolve the conflict between these two women.

This leader is to "help" them live in harmony with each other. A third party is needed to reconcile them. "Help" (*sullambano*) is a strong, active word in the Greek, meaning "to seize, to grasp, to apprehend." It can also mean "to arrest, to capture, to take hold of." This word was used for the arrest of Jesus Christ by the Roman soldiers (Mark 14:48). It was also used of the arrest of Peter, when he was arrested and imprisoned (Acts 12:3). So in Philippians, Paul is telling this person to take hold of this situation and usher in peace between the two women.

Paul addresses them positively, as those who "shared my struggle in the cause of the gospel" (Philippians **4:3**). They had worked in the ministry with Paul, whether by praying for him, encouraging him, giving to him or showing him hospitality. We do not know how they shared in Paul's struggle, but we do know that they did. All the more reason, then, why they needed to be reconciled. In their struggle with Paul for the gospel, we see their commitment to the work of God. They were strong in convictions, personality, actions, and involvement in God's work. We can assume that, given these characters, when they clashed, they were also strong in their difficulties with one another.

Paul mentions another person by name: "Clement" (**verse 3**). We do not know who Clement is, but he was obviously a well-known man in the church with spiritual influence. He is cited here as working with these women, "and the rest of my fellow workers." This is the team spirit that characterized this church in Philippi. They were all involved together. These believers were not a series of islands, disconnected from each other, each person doing their own thing. Instead, they were shouldering the ministering load together, standing as one in the cause of the gospel. Consequently, the breach between these two women was affecting everyone in this tightly-knit church.

Paul concludes by underlining that the **protagonists'** "names are in the book of life." This is to underscore that these are true believers who are in conflict. The Philippians are not to conclude that these women are unbelievers. To the contrary, their names are in the book of life, having been chosen by the Father before time began. These are sisters in the Lord, who must now work this out.

Rejoicing Despite the Conflict

It is in light of the conflict he has just addressed that we should understand what Paul says next: "Rejoice in the Lord always; again I will say, rejoice!" (**v 4**). In spite of the friction between Euodia and Syntyche and the two sides they represent, Paul urges the believers to rejoice in the midst of this conflict. Such a dispute can make rejoicing seem impossible. However, Paul urges the believers to rejoice nonetheless.

This verse expresses the central theme of the book of Philippians, which is a call to believers to rejoice no matter what the circumstances are. So important to Christian living is rejoicing that Paul repeats this command for emphasis. At this time, it is a challenge to rejoice, given the turbulence created by these two women, who were unreconciled. "Rejoice" is a present imperative verb, a command that requires continual, habitual rejoicing. These in-house differences and disagreements should not prevent the Philippians from rejoicing. Most likely, rejoicing together may serve to heal the divide. Rejoicing in all the Lord is to us and for us has the habit of introducing the correct perspective on everything else, especially in conflict.

In other words, their circumstances may cause them to be saddened or less than joyful. After all, they should be grieved by what grieves the heart of God. Nevertheless, they can rejoice in who God is as well as in what he has done, is doing, and will do on their behalf. This understanding of God will have a direct effect upon their experience of joy. Fee points out that…

"'Joy' unmitigated, untrammeled joy, is—or at least should be— the distinctive mark of the believer in Christ Jesus. The wearing of black and the long face, which so often came to typify some later expressions of Christian piety, are totally foreign to the Pauline version." (*Paul's Letter to the Philippians*, page 404)

A high view of God produces overflowing joy, but a low view of him yields little joy.

Living Gently

Given that this conflict exists, Paul makes this appeal, "Let your gentle spirit be known to all men" (**v 5**). In the midst of this relational storm, the believers in the church should not allow their emotions to escalate and intensify and so become angry at others, possibly reacting harshly to one another. Such times of friction can bring the worst out of people. Instead, they should show a "gentle spirit." "Gentle" (*epieikes*) means to be mild in reacting to another. This is a call for patience with those who would otherwise provoke a response of anger. It is a call to overlook the faults of others. "A gentle answer turns away wrath, but a harsh word stirs up anger" (Proverbs 15:1).

This gentle spirit must be shown "to all men" (Philippians **4:5**). The intent is probably that the Philippians should demonstrate loving patience to all who are being polarized in the church. Of course, such gentleness must also be exhibited toward unbelievers outside the church, but given the context, Paul's appeal is surely directed toward the believers inside the church who are being pulled into the dispute between these two women. They must show a level-headed response to all involved.

The Lord Is Close

To conclude this section, Paul reminds the church that "the Lord is near" (**v 5**). This is not a statement concerning the second coming of Christ. Rather, this is an affirmation that the Lord is near to his people in order to give his joy to troubled hearts. The Lord is present as reconciliation between these two disputing women is sought. This is a simple reminder of Christ's closeness to his people in a time of unrest, to grant his peace and to calm hearts.

Such closeness by the Lord to his people is a reminder that all believers need. Jesus assured his disciples, "I am with you always, even to the end of the age" (Matthew 28:20). This is what the Lord spoke to Paul amid his difficulties in Corinth: "I am with you" (Acts 18:10). God plus one always makes a majority. David testified, "The LORD is near to the brokenhearted" (Psalm 34:18). Asaph took comfort in this truth: "The nearness of God is my good" (Psalm 73:28). This is the point that Paul is making with the Philippians.

> Those who will spend an eternity in joyful unity ought to start living in it now.

As we find ourselves in situations of strife between believers, let us respond with a gentle spirit. A harsh word only provokes anger. Instead, let us be peacemakers who take confidence in the closeness of God to reconcile disputing people and parties. Conflicts will come, for the church is a collection of sinners—saved sinners, but selfish sinners nonetheless. But conflicts must be taken seriously, and confronted by those involved and those around. When conflict occurs between believers, by definition what they have in common in the Lord is always greater than anything that is driving them apart; and those who will spend an eternity in joyful unity and peace ought to start living in it now. May the Lord draw near and maintain the unity of the Spirit in the bond of peace.

Questions for reflection

1. How does rejoicing together pull us out of conflict with each other?

2. In what sense should joy and grief co-exist within Christians? Which are you more prone to neglect or suppress?

3. "The Lord is near." With what in particular do you need his help today? With what in particular does your church need his help today?

13. PEACE OF MIND

Though Paul is imprisoned in Rome, he is a man who knows peace. He is in chains, attached to a Roman soldier, twenty-four hours a day, seven days a week, and he has been in this situation for two long years.

This man previously lived an adventurous life, traveling from city to city; now, he goes nowhere. He has restricted movement, limited resources, and dwindling support. This industrious, fast-paced preacher, who was constantly active and moving about, is now confined under house arrest.

Nevertheless, the message that comes from this imprisoned man is not that of a chronic worrier. He is not replaying the circumstances of his life, wondering how he got into this trial, and how he might escape it. Instead, this is a man who knows peace in his heart despite his circumstances. In the midst of the storm raging around him, a tranquil calm has settled into his heart. Paul, who has many reasons to feel conflicted and anxious, is a man who is at peace. We have much to learn from him.

While Paul was chained in prison, the Philippians had ministered to him by sending financial support (4:18). They sent the offering to him by way of a messenger. So Paul writes back; the book of Philippians is in reality a thank-you letter to express his gratitude for their gift. So, given the Philippians' concern for Paul, this would seem to be the perfect time for Paul to be transparent and indicate that he is collapsing on the inside. But the apostle does not respond this way. Instead, he urges them to commit their burdens to the Lord in prayer—because, undoubtedly, this is what he himself has been doing, and it has brought a calming stillness to his own soul.

The Philippians had ministered to Paul, and now he is ministering to them through this letter. He encourages them to not be anxious for him or anything else they might encounter personally. Rather, they must commit every concern to God in prayer and focus their minds upon what is pure. The result will be that God's peace will flood their minds and hearts. As we look at these verses, Paul will minister to us as well, in how we handle circumstances that may cause us worry today.

No Need to Panic

Paul instructs the Philippians to avoid being anxious in their Christian lives. "Be anxious for nothing" (**v 6**). In other words, *Stop being anxious.* Put another way, *Stop worrying.* "Anxious" (*merimnao*) means to be troubled with cares. The idea is literally to be pulled in different directions, or to be pulled apart. The picture is to suffer the tension of your hopes pulling in one direction and the trials of life pulling in the opposite direction. The person in such a situation feels like he is being pulled apart and is at breaking point.

"Worry" comes from an old English word meaning "to strangle." This is a good image, because stress chokes our inner life (and sometimes the way we feel physically), robbing us of peace. Worry squeezes the life out of the heart, strangling all enjoyment of life. To be anxious is to be a worrier, to be fearful and distressed; and such anxiety compromises our faith in the sovereign purposes of God. And in that way, anxiety robs us of our joy.

When Paul says, "Be anxious for nothing," this is a command. Though it may be strange to think of it like this, to be anxious is to be disobedient to God. Worry is a failure to trust that God is in control. It reveals that we are not sure that God will provide what we need in his perfect timing. Worry is gazing at my problems in self-reliance or self-pity or both, rather than looking to the Lord in dependence. Worry is the failure to believe the promises of God in his word. This does not mean that we should not be concerned about issues in our lives in the midst of difficulties. Yet Paul stresses that believers must not be pulled apart and strangled of peace and joy—we must not be anxious and worried.

Jesus taught the same: "Do not be worried about your life, as to what you will eat or what you will drink; nor for your body, as to what you will put on" (Matthew 6:25). He is saying, *Stop being worried.* Instead, trust God who will provide for your needs. It is

> What causes you panic? There is no panic in heaven, only plans to work out God's good purposes in your life.

worth asking yourself: what is there in my life that causes me a sense of panic, either low-level or almost paralyzing? Realize that God is not worried. There is no panic in heaven, but only plans to work out his good purposes in your life. There is no need to worry. There is no excuse for worry. "Do not worry" is both a command to trust the Lord and an invitation to enjoy peace with the Lord.

The Primary Cure for Worry

So how do we live without anxiety? There is one primary cure for worry, and that is prayer: "In everything by prayer and supplication with thanksgiving let your requests be made known to God" (Philippians **4:6**). In this context, these prayers address whatever is causing the anxiety and stealing our peace of mind. Notice the stark contrast between "everything" and "nothing"—the believer is to be anxious for "nothing," but praying about "everything." "Everything" carries the idea of every troubling situation that threatens the peace of God. Paul uses four words for prayer, each making a unique contribution to its comprehensive nature: "prayer," "supplication," "thanksgiving," and "requests."

The first word, "prayer," is the most general term for intercession to God. It is the standard word that encompasses all of the different elements that should to go into prayer. The second, "supplication," comes from a root word which means "to lack" or "to be deprived of," or "to be without something." The specific areas in which we lack something will naturally create stress and worry. Instead, we are to bring our concerns about what we are lacking to the Lord. We should trust that God will answer the prayer and meet our need according to his perfect will. The third, "thanksgiving," must also be a part of our prayers. All true prayer will be marked by gratitude. At the same time as recognizing what we are lacking, we must also acknowledge what God has provided for us. No matter how dire our circumstances, he has lavished his blessing upon his children. So his children must constantly pray, ask, and offer thanksgiving. There is no shortcut to peace. But prayer is the path to it.

The fourth word is "requests," which instructs us to make known to God the specific needs we have. We should bring our particular requests to him, whatever is troubling us. Bringing specific requests to God is illustrated in the parable Jesus told about prayer (Luke 11:5-8). A person who is hosting a friend, but lacks food to feed him, goes to another person to seek what is needed. This host asks not merely for food, but specifically, for bread. Moreover he asks specifically for three loaves. He makes specific requests and receives what he needs. So it should be that believers bring similar requests to God in prayer.

What are the specific needs in your life? What has been weighing you down? What is burdening you? What has become a millstone around your neck? What is dragging you down? Here is the ground where anxiety will flourish, if unchecked and unchallenged. But this also is the ground where dependence, trust and joy may grow, if you pursue dependent prayer. Will you bring your requests to the Lord in prayer?

Enjoying Peace

No matter how your prayer is answered, taking your concerns to God in prayer brings his abundant, supernatural peace: "And the peace of God, which surpasses all comprehension, will guard your hearts and your minds in Christ Jesus" (Philippians **4:7**). God himself is peace (Romans 16:20; Ephesians 2:14). That is, all peace exclusively belongs to him alone. Therefore, he alone can give peace. "Peace" (*eirene*) is an inner tranquility of soul. It is an inner calm that settles the turbulence of troubled hearts. The result of casting our burdens on the Lord is to be unstressed and undisturbed; or, as Paul says, to know a peace that "surpasses all comprehension" (Philippians **4:7**)—that is, it exceeds human comprehension or explanation. Motyer explains what Paul means here:

> "Our lives will be touched with a mark of the supernatural, something that passes all understanding (**v 7**). The meaning here is not of something mysterious and incomprehensible in its own right, but of something which man cannot explain or explain away; something which runs beyond the range of human comprehension." (*The Message of Philippians,* pages 207-208)

There is no explanation for this peace except that God provides it. It is a supernatural peace that is unnatural, flooding the heart, and drowning out worry. When a believer prays, God may not change their circumstances, but he does change their heart.

This peace, Paul explains, will "guard" the heart and mind (**v 7**). "Guard" (*phroureo*) is a military term describing a soldier who watches over a prisoner. Paul was being guarded by praetorian guards, the most elite soldiers in the Roman empire. However, he was also being guarded in a far more secure way—God was protecting his heart so that anxiety and fear would not enter it. Fear was being denied entrance into his heart. When preceded by prayer, the peace of God is always standing watch like a sentry over "your hearts and your minds in Christ Jesus" (**v 7**). The entire inner person is being fortified against the attacks of worry, and anxiety cannot crack the divine defense. The Christian who prays dependently is guarded against the enemy of worry.

Paul specifies that this peace is found "in Christ Jesus." This supernatural peace of Christ is all-sufficient, even in the most turbulent storms of life. Jesus had promised, "Peace I leave with you; My peace I give to you; not as the world gives do I give to you. Do not let your heart be troubled, nor let it be fearful" (John 14:27). This peace comes not from this world or anything in it. Instead, it comes down from above, like a surging river into troubled hearts, and such peace is found exclusively in Christ Jesus. There is not a drop of genuine peace outside of him, nor a moment of relief apart from resting in him. All peace and all comfort are found in Christ, and in him alone.

Are you experiencing this peace? Do you need this kind of inner tranquility? It is found exclusively in trusting Jesus Christ and is obtained through prayer. We must come before his throne of grace and pray. We must commit our problems and our trials to the Lord. He supplies a perfect peace that is unexplainable and incomprehensible. If you are outside of Christ, you actually have much reason to worry—more than you realize if you consider eternity. But if you will come to him, he will receive you and forgive you, and you will become the recipient of his abiding peace, which is experienced only in life with him, and is elusive when sought anywhere else and in anything else.

Questions for reflection

1. What are the three main sources of your anxiety today, and how does that anxiety manifest itself in your emotions and your life? How attractive do you find the idea of knowing peace about those things?

2. Have you ever considered, or accepted, that "worry is the failure to believe the promises of God in his word"? Why is it easy to decide that this does not apply to *our* particular worries?

3. How will you apply the cure for worry that Paul lays out in these verses to your anxieties?

PART TWO

In Philippians **4:8**, Paul reaches the climax of his appeal. "Finally, brethren…" he writes—directing this to all the believers in Philippi, and to every believer in every place. What follows is not merely for some Christians. This is not reserved only for those whose conscience is unusually sensitive or those who are naturally emotional. Instead, this is addressed to all Christians, all who are born into God's family. None of us are above this and no one is excluded from this.

The Focus of Your Attention

Paul prioritizes the mind: "Dwell on these things" (**v 8**). "Dwell on" means to think about, to be focused upon mentally. The Philippians must focus upon those things that are worthy of their thought. "Dwell" (*logizomai*) has come into the English language as "logarithms" and "logic." This is a mathematical term and carries the idea of making a careful calculation, requiring great concentration. The word means to reckon, to evaluate, to consider, to take into account, and conveys the idea of thinking carefully about something. The Philippians must mentally focus and intellectually dwell upon certain things which are lawful and proper.

"Dwell on" is in the present tense, meaning that they should always be thinking on these things. There is never a day off from the requirement to do this. Further, it is in the active voice, indicating they must take action to dwell on these things. And notice that it is an imperative—this is an apostolic command issued with divine authority.

If we focus upon what is right, we will live rightly. Conversely, if we focus upon what is wrong, we will live wrongly. There is this inseparable connection between what we think about and how we live. Right thoughts produce right living, just as wrong thoughts produce wrong living. We cannot focus our minds on what is wrong and then live out what is right. The deposits that are being made into our minds are yielding a return with interest in our lives. As MacArthur points out:

"Spiritual stability is a result of how a person thinks ... The Bible leaves no doubt that people's lives are the product of their thoughts." (*The MacArthur New Testament Commentary on Philippians,* page 285)

In these next words, Paul will provide timeless, transcendent principles that stretch over the centuries, that stretch over the cultures, and that stretch over the continents, that are applicable and relevant for every one of us here today. With each one of these descriptions, he is putting a fence around that which we ought to be allowing in our minds.

What to Dwell On

Here is the requirement for the peace that God establishes: "Whatever is true, whatever is honorable, whatever is right, whatever is pure, whatever is lovely, whatever is of good repute, if there is any excellence and if anything worthy of praise, dwell on these things" (**v 8**). Paul catalogs eight godly objects upon which Christians must concentrate, and so believers must discipline their minds to think upon these spiritual subjects.

1. "Whatever is true." "True" (*alethes*) means that which is reliable and faithful, distinguished from what is false or a lie. That is, their minds need to be fixed upon on whatever is real, genuine, authentic. What is true is found in, or aligns with, the word of God. "Whatever is true" is defined by the Scripture. Whenever the Bible says something, it is real. Focusing upon what is true leads to true Christianity. Equally, dwelling upon what is the antithesis of truth produces false living.

2. "Whatever is honorable." "Honorable" (*semnos*) means that which is noble, dignified, lofty, elevated, venerable, august. It represents that which is of high and lofty morality. They must set their thoughts on elevated things. They should think about that which pulls them up, and not what takes them down. They should think about those things that pull them above the muck and mire of

this world. They should concentrate upon those things that are principled, decent, and upright. Paul is saying, *Get your mind off of low and base things. Get your mind out of the gutter. Get your attention off frivolous things. Focus on the honorable.* In a culture today that is continuously more and more casual, focusing on that which is honorable is truly a biblical virtue.

3. "Whatever is right." "Right" (*dikaios*) means that which is upright and holy, which conforms to the law of God. In ancient times, this word was used of scales in the marketplace. A standardized measure would be placed on one side of the scales and an amount of grain of equal measure would be poured onto the other side until the scales were balanced. At that point they would be said to be "right." That is the idea here. On one side of the scales of Christian living is the holiness of God and on the other side is what a believer focuses his mind upon. Whatever a believer thinks about needs to square with the absolute purity of God. His thoughts must be in conformity with God's word.

4. "Whatever is pure." "Pure" (*hagnos*) comes from the root word for holy, holiness, and sanctification. This word refers to what is unmixed with moral impurities and is set apart to be ethically clean. It is what is unmixed with filth or adulterated with moral corruption. The Philippians should fill their minds with whatever is morally pure. They should think upon whatever is wholesome, virtuous, and unstained by corruption. There should be censorship in every Christian mind. If we are to live a pure life—that is, an unstained, Christ-like life—our minds must dwell upon what is pure.

5. "Whatever is lovely." "Lovely" (*prosphiles*) speaks of that which is pleasing, attractive, and beautiful, which reflects ethical beauty. This word refers to the beauty of holiness, as opposed to the hideousness of sin. "Lovely" represents that which is sweet, gracious, and generous. This is the opposite of what is raw, crude, and ugly. Whatever is "lovely" is that which is beautiful in the eyes of God and spiritually attractive to those who are pure in heart. In this

way, believers must direct their thoughts onto what the Bible says is pleasing to God. He defines what is attractive—not us, and not the world. The world very often hangs something unlovely on a bait marked "Lovely." So Christians must make every effort to remain focused upon that which is truly "lovely," which is defined for us in the Scriptures.

6. "Whatever is of good repute." "Good repute" (*euphemus*) means that which is well spoken of or highly regarded. This idea refers to whatever is well spoken of by God. It is that which is highly respectable in the eyes of God. Paul warns about the negative aspect of this in his letter to the Ephesians: "There must be no filthiness and silly talk, or coarse jesting, which are not fitting, but rather giving of thanks." (Ephesians 5:4). These forbidden things are not fitting for any believer who is pursuing holiness. Instead, those with a high and holy calling upon their lives should be dwelling upon what is morally respectable.

7. "If there is any excellence," Christians should dwell on this. "If there is" starts a bottom-line summary. "Excellence" means mental virtue. Only that which reflects high moral standards should dominate our thinking. Whatever reflects the holiness of Almighty God, that which is morally excellent and pleasing, should fill our minds and occupy our thoughts. If we dwell upon that which is excellent, we will live a spiritually excellent life. Our affections then will be consumed with his perfect and pleasing will (Romans 12:2), and it all starts at the highest level, with the mind.

8. "Anything worthy of praise." This encompasses whatever is or can be praised by God. It means we should think about whatever can be applauded in the presence of God. Christians focus their thoughts upon only whatever can be commended by God. Put another way, this is whatever can be extolled by the holiness of Almighty God. Let the minds of believers be set upon these things.

These eight marks define what should saturate our thinking. Ultimately, each of these virtues is a description of the Lord Jesus Christ. This is how he thought, constantly and consistently, in every circumstance and at every point. And so whatever meets this mark is acceptable and pleasing to God, but whatever falls short of this standard is unacceptable. We must guard our minds because we will soon become like that upon which we are thinking.

Practicing What He Has Preached

How do we put these defining marks into practice? One way is by seeing them lived out in the life of a more mature believer. This is why Paul says next, "The things you have learned and received and heard and seen in me, practice these things, and the God of peace will be with you" (Philippians **4:9**). There is a direct connection between what is required in **verse 8** and what Paul urges in **verse 9**. As the Philippians strive to dwell on what is acceptable, they should look to Paul and emulate him.

In **verse 9**, Paul gives four ways they should put into practice what Paul has prescribed in the preceding verse:

■ *Things Learned:* Paul first urges them to imitate "the things you have learned." This refers to what Paul had taught them and preached to them when he was in Philippi. The focus is upon the truth that he expounded and the sound doctrine they learned. This underscores the importance for every Christian to sit under sound Bible teaching and preaching, just as the Philippians had.

■ *Things Received:* These same truths were also taught to the Philippians in the things they "received." This refers to what Paul wrote to them in this epistle. Here is the importance of the public reading of Scripture in church. Paul intended that the written word of God be read to the people of God in their corporate gatherings (Colossians 4:16; 1 Thessalonians 5:27). The same can be said for studying its truths. This demonstrates the necessity of hearing and receiving the sanctifying truth of Scripture by reading its message.

■ *Things Heard:* There was also "the things you have ... heard" (Philippians **4:9**). This refers to what they heard from others about Paul. It includes the reports of those who were with Paul and observed in his life, especially while he was in prison. How was Paul responding to this Roman imprisonment in which he found himself? How was Paul reacting to the unjust suffering? How was he leaving this matter in the hands of God? Was he turning the other cheek? Was he responding with grace to those who would curse him? Was Paul anxious and worried, or filled with peace? That news spread like wildfire, and it came all the way to Philippi. The reports that they heard about Paul's Roman imprisonment and how he was living his life were a powerful teaching tool.

■ *Things Seen:* Paul says that they should practice what they have "seen" in him. This points to those things that Paul modeled when in their presence. Here is what they directly observed in Paul's life. They were to remember how he walked in the faith, how he handled himself, and how he acted and reacted. In every situation, this was an aid for them in living a godly life in Christ. To follow what they had seen in Paul allowed them to be imitations of him, and ultimately of Christ.

Paul writes, "Practice these things" (**v 9**). The word "practice" (*passo*) means to do, to execute, to perform. This is an imperative—a command. It is in the present tense, indicating it is to be an ongoing pursuit in their lives. Paul is saying, *You need to live in a manner consistent with my life and with my teaching.* Paul has modeled his own message and has become a visible example to the Philippians concerning how they should live in their pursuit of holiness.

This is the principle of discipleship. Jesus taught that "a pupil is not above his teacher; but everyone, after he has been fully trained, will be like his teacher" (Luke 6:40). In like manner, Paul urged, "I exhort you, be imitators of me" (1 Corinthians 4:16). And this is Paul's command for these Philippian believers: *The things you have seen and learned from me, now go do them in your own lives.*

The Battle of the Mind

What is the result of efforts to dwell upon what is holy? "The God of peace will be with you" (Philippians **4:9**). So, purity of mind is essential for peace of heart. Verse 9 is inseparably connected to the verse that precedes it. "Peace" here refers to the subjective peace of God, and not the objective peace with God that comes through being justified by him (Romans 5:1). Peace in the heart can only come from God. It is part of the fruit of the Spirit (Galatians 5:22) that Christ gives (John 14:27). *God is with you,* Paul writes, *to give you his peace.*

It is impossible to overestimate the importance of a pure mind that is kept undefiled by the impurities of this world. Wherever a life is growing spiritually, there is always a pure mind. An impure mind not only stunts Christian growth, but is contrary to the will of God for our lives.

In many ways, the battle of the Christian life is a battle of the mind. And the victory in the battle is the experience of peace. Prayer and purity are the two keys to the life of peace.

> You will become in practice what fills your mind in thought.

You will become in practice what fills your mind in thought. Godly thoughts will produce godly living. Holy thinking will lead to holy living. Conversely, base thoughts will lead to base living, so it is critical that we guard our minds from impurity. We must set our minds on the written word of God, dwelling upon Jesus Christ. We must notice and censor those thoughts that are not pure, policing the borders of our lives ruthlessly. This is every believer's responsibility. It does not just happen without effort. If we are to live in a distinctly pure way, we must intentionally set our minds on what is pure.

Like produces like in the battle for the mind. So be careful what you allow behind the steering wheel of your mind because either it will take you where you do not intend to go or drive you deeper into the peace of knowing and obeying the Lord.

Questions for reflection

Reflect on the eight areas to "dwell on" laid out on pages 200-202. For each...

1. To what extent are you already thinking this way?

2. Are there ways you are failing to think like this? What are you dwelling on instead?

3. How will you pursue godly thinking more proactively?

14. CONTENT IN CRISIS

As we consider Paul's words in these verses, as so often with this letter, we need to remember that his circumstances are anything but good. The apostle is imprisoned in Rome, chained to the elite Roman guards who serve in Caesar's household. He is awaiting trial before Caesar with his own life at stake, confined under house arrest, and unable to move about with freedom. As for any active man, being shut up under house arrest in chains for two years must have made him feel like a caged lion held against his will.

To make matters worse, the local pastors in Rome have become so envious of Paul's giftedness that they have resorted to a smear campaign against him. His reputation has come under attack as he is now held captive. To add insult to injury, he is forced to pay his own rent for his house arrest (Acts 28:30). When the church at Philippi received word of his desperate plight, they took up a gift to pay for Paul's imprisonment and gave it to Epaphroditus to bring to him in Rome. But this man sent to minister to him had, as we have seen, become sick almost to the point of death. Whatever could go wrong appears to have gone wrong.

However, as Paul writes this letter, his words have the vibrant tone of a man sitting in a palace, not a prison. The apostle is not defeated in spirit, but instead he is a triumphant, joyful man who, rather than needing to be encouraged, is lifting up others. Paul writes to express his gratitude for the generosity of the Philippians in ministering to his needs. Here is what it looks like for a believer to live above his circumstances, and not under them. Paul is a man who is content despite his circumstances, rather than being crushed by them.

Paul's Celebration

Though Paul is in prison in Rome, an unsuspecting reader of this letter would not know it. As MacArthur points out:

"Though his situation was extremely difficult, Paul was not discontent. It did not matter that he was a prisoner, living in a small apartment, chained to a Roman soldier, subsisting on a sparse diet. None of that affected his contentment."

(*The MacArthur New Testament Commentary on Philippians,* page 299)

Paul writes, "But I rejoiced in the Lord greatly" (Philippians **4:10**). Paul does not lament his position but instead is a man fully of joy.

> Genuine joy is not dictated by your changing circumstances; it is found in the unchangeable Lord.

As noted earlier, a great difference exists between happiness and joy. Happiness is dependent upon what is happening in your life. However, genuine joy is not dictated by your changing circumstances. Genuine joy is found in the unchangeable Lord. When Paul states, "I rejoiced in the Lord greatly," he is saying that the Lord is the source and sphere of his joy.

He is rejoicing in the greatness of the Lord's all-wise providence in his life. He is rejoicing in his all-sufficient provision for him. He knows that God is causing all things to work together for good—even this imprisonment (Romans 8:28).

Though life's affairs are always changing, the eternal purposes of God never change. Paul realizes that he is in chains by divine appointment, and because of that he has every reason to rejoice.

This joy that Paul is experiencing is not derived from this world, but comes from God. Joy comes down from above, from the throne of grace. Paul had always wanted to go to Rome and preach the gospel; he had just never envisioned that it would be under these circumstances. He has gone through arrest, trials, and shipwreck and he is now confined, sitting in prison. Nevertheless, he "greatly" rejoices! This is not simply a little joy that he has, but joy in abundant supply.

Paul rejoices "that now at last you have revived your concern for me" (Philippians **4:10**). Here he gives some insight as to what has triggered this joy. He is grateful that God has met his needs through the generosity of the Philippians. Paul knows that it is God working in them in their ministry to him. He knows that God is at work for his good pleasure in these brothers and sisters (2:13). It is God who has revived this concern for him in them, this desire to help him, and Paul is certain that this is the result of God at work in their lives.

To review, Paul first came to Philippi ten years earlier, a full decade prior (Acts 16). When Paul was there, he preached the gospel, won souls to Christ, and planted a church. When Paul left town, he traveled to Athens and then to Corinth. They continued to give support to Paul for his ministry. There is no record of their involvement with him in the years that followed. After many years, as we see here, they have revived their concern for him. The reference here is to the financial gift they sent, mentioned in Philippians 4:18. "Revived" (*anathallo*) is a horticultural term that was used to describe a plant that had been blossoming, and went dormant for the winter, but then sprouted new, green growth at springtime. So it was in Paul's relationship with the Philippians. There had, it seems, been a long winter in their relationship, but now they have re-sprouted their concern for him and, subsequently, their generosity in giving to him.

Paul explains, "You were concerned before, but you lacked opportunity" (**v 10**). This looks back to a time after their initial support when they (Paul generously assumes) lacked the means to continue supporting him. Paul has expressed his gratitude in a gracious manner. He does not want to appear to be unthankful for the time when they did not support him. He does not question where their support has been or why it has been withheld. Perhaps the reason remained unstated to shield the Philippians from public embarrassment. Maybe they were without the financial resources necessary. Maybe they did not have a way to send the money to him. Maybe there were political hindrances that prevented a gift going to him. We do not know what caused the lack of opportunity.

Paul's attitude is an example to every Christian. Let us not be dependent upon our happenings for our joy, but rejoice in the Lord and be quick to see his hand at work for our good. And let us assume the best of our Christian brothers and sisters. All our joy comes from God. Our joy abounds in fellowship with his people. May we look to him, for there is not one drop of true joy to be found in this world.

Paul's Contentment

But still, we must ask, how can Paul be rejoicing in the midst of imprisonment? How can he know gladness while being unjustly treated as a common criminal? The answer is found in what follows: "Not that I speak from want, for I have learned to be content in whatever circumstances I am" (**v 11**). This is a staggering statement for Paul to make, given where he is and what he is suffering. Paul can say, *All my needs are met.* "Not that I speak from want, for I have learned…" Let us just stop right there.

What Paul learned is what you and I must learn. Paul did not learn this sitting at the feet of Gamaliel, the rabbi who schooled him in Judaism (Acts 22:3). He did not learn this by receiving one of the greatest educations in that part of the known world. He did not learn this as a Pharisee of Pharisees. This is something that he had to learn in the school of discipleship with Christ. As experience reveals, this is usually learned not in times of prosperity but adversity. This is a valuable lesson that Paul has learned, and that we would do well also to learn.

When Paul writes, "I have learned to be content" (Philippians **4:11**), this speaks of a calm acceptance of his present lot in life. To be discontent would mean that Paul wants to be somewhere else than where the sovereign hand of God has placed him, and to have more than the sovereign hand of God has chosen to give him. To be content is to have a peaceful acceptance of where God has providentially placed him. "Content" (*autarkes*) was used of a country that had everything that it needed and where nothing had to be imported. Such a country had all the resources and natural products needed to be self-sufficient. Nothing else was needed from the outside.

Of course, Paul is not saying that he is self-sufficient in himself. Rather, he is abundantly sufficient in the resources of God. Nothing needs to be imported from outside his life. There is nothing lacking from the ample supply provided by Christ living within him. Paul has everything that he needs in the fullness of his Savior and Lord. No matter what the situation is, Paul has learned to be content. He is independent of anything external; no outside aid is necessary for his Christian life. This is a remarkable statement of the all-sufficiency found in Jesus Christ. This is the secret of contentment.

Questions for reflection

1. To what extent is joy the emotional response to contentment?

2. Where do people look for contentment? What brings you contentment?

3. How do we lose Christian contentment if we forget either that God is sovereign, or that God is good?

PART TWO

"I have learned to be content in whatever circumstances I am" (**v 11**). *Whether my circumstances are good or bad, up or down, positive or painful*, Paul says, *I am content*. Now in **verse 12**, he fleshes this out a little bit more, and he certainly gets my attention, because I am still learning this. Paul has got a hold of something here that you and I desperately need. None of us are above or beyond what he says; rather, all of us are in need of this important truth.

Paul begins **verse 12**, "I know…" Let us just stop right there. Paul knows this because Paul has learned this; it is what he told us in **verse 11**. Paul has learned this by personal experience of trusting God in hard times. He says, "I know how to get along" (**v 12**) and when he says "get along" he means how to get along joyfully, triumphantly, successfully—not just surviving, but thriving. He says, "I know how to get along with humble means." We can be sure of this because Paul is living in the lap of humble means as he writes this. You would be hard pressed to be more humble in means than Paul is right now. He faces a low supply of provisions, financial shortage, physical affliction, restricted movement, and limited food. Yet despite this trial, Paul is abounding in Christ.

Paul also writes, "I also know how to live in prosperity." The word "prosperity" means to be filled with an abundance. The idea is one of being furnished with more than is needed. There have been other times in Paul's life when this was the case, when he sat in the lap of luxury. In those seasons, he had more provisions than he needed. But part of the secret of contentment he has learned is that, when in a time of prosperity, his contentment still does not come from that source. That would be a pale contentment that looks to circumstances, however good. Paul did not look for contentment in Christ only when he lacked other things to give it him; he sought contentment in Christ in want and in plenty.

Paul has learned to be content "in any and every circumstance," whether he is in prosperity or in prison. In every situation, he has lived triumphantly: "I have learned the secret of being filled and go-ing hungry, both of having abundance and suffering need" (**v 12**). He says again, "I have learned…" This is not mere head knowledge, but a heart experience born out of real situations. He claims to know the secret to this. "Secret" (*mueo*) is a word which means to be initiated in mysteries. In Paul's day, it referred to the initiation rites into a mys-tery religion. When someone entered into one of the pagan temples to be a part of those mystery religions, there would be an initiation process in which secrets would be made known to that person. They were not made known to the average person on the streets. But, as Hendriksen explains, the only "initiation" necessary to learn this secret is to fear and trust in God:

> "To those who fear him God reveals this mystery (Psalm 25:14).
> Those who reject Christ cannot understand how it is possible for
> a Christian to remain calm in adversity, humble in prosperity."
>
> (*Philippians*, page 205)

"Filled" means for your stomach to be full with food, or for your pock-etbook to be filled with all that is needed. You can be satisfied when filled, but also when hungry, when both your stomach and pocket are empty. These two extreme circumstances are polar opposites. They are at either end of the spectrum of life; Paul is putting his arms around the entirety of human experience. This is a literary device known as inclu-sion, and implies every other life experience in between. When "having abundance," Paul had more than he needed. When he was "suffering need," he did not have anything, either physically or financially. Every-thing else he or we may experience lies somewhere in between.

The Secret of Contentment

So then, what is this secret of contentment? Here is the mystery that Paul learned in the school of discipleship. In the difficult times of life, Paul thrived, as he discovered that "I can do all things through Him who strengthens me" (Philippians **4:13**). "All things" is put in the emphatic position in Paul's original sentence order. The word order is, "All things

I can do." It is as if Paul took a yellow highlighter and underscored the two words "all things." These two words are what should leap off the page. But additionally, Paul does not say, *I may do all things,* but "I *can* do…" A world of difference exists between "may" and "can." "May" indicates permission, but "can" means ability.

Further, as Hansen points out:

"The contextual meaning of 'all' refers to the previous claim to be content whatever the circumstances (**4:11**). In all the situations of his life—in poverty and in prosperity, when well fed and when hungry, Paul can be content. He has the power to endure all these extreme situations, all these ups and downs, without anxiety, with the peace of God guarding his heart and mind in Christ Jesus (4:6-7)." (*The Letter to the Philippians,* page 314)

The word "do" (*ischuo*) means to be strong, to have power. It conveys the idea of having strength to perform a task. In Acts 19:16, the word is translated as "overpowered." Paul states emphatically that he possesses the power to do all things. This refers to all things within the will of God—all things that glorify God.

> It is as if Paul took a yellow highlighter and underscored the words *all things.*

The little phrase "through Him" refers to the Lord Jesus Christ—the One who is the object of Paul's faith is the One who gives him the power to do everything that God has called him to do. Paul's whole life is Christ (Philippians 1:21), and it is through him that Paul possesses all the strength that he needs for his life. Jesus said, "Apart from Me you can do nothing" (John 15:5). Paul has discovered that, in him, he can do everything.

The word "strengthens" is the word that comes into our English language as dynamite. It means to be empowered, to be enabled, to be made strong, to be increased in strength. I can do all things through Christ who strengthens me. This is as individual and personal as it can be. No matter what anyone else is doing—in your family, at work, in your church—this confidence is individual and personal. You can do all things through the strength of the Lord Jesus Christ in the midst of your personally difficult circumstances.

Misunderstood and Misapplied

This verse has, however, been misunderstood, and misapplied, repeatedly over time. So it needs some qualification:

1. First, this does not mean God will empower me to sin. God is not the author of sin. That comes from the flesh. "All things" would never include that which God hates or that which is opposed to his very nature.

2. Second, this does not mean I can do supernatural physical feats, such as jump across the Atlantic Ocean or flap my arms and fly to the moon. It does not mean I can perform miracles. "All things" are the simple things of life that all believers are called to do.

3. Third, this means I can do all things within the will of God. I can do all things that God calls me to do. We must understand "all things" as everything that is defined by the word of God.

4. Fourth, this does not relieve me of my responsibility to commit myself to the means of grace—God's word, God's meal at the Lord's Supper, and so on. In other words, if I just sit back passively, I am not going to know this strength. It requires my active pursuit of the means of grace for me to experience this supernatural power in my life.

5. Fifth, this does not remove my responsibility to confess our sin and to repent. If there is unconfessed, unrepentant sin in your life, it will pull the plug on your joy. Sin and joy cannot coexist in the same heart. Of course, we will never be perfect, and there will always be sin in our lives, but if there are patterns of sin going on in my life, no matter how good my circumstances happen to be, there is no joy.

6. Sixth, this does mean that as I can live my Christian life knowing that the power of God is far greater than whatever the difficulty is that I am facing. There is no trial too difficult. There is no obstacle too high. There is no temptation too strong. There is no opposition too powerful. There is no persecution too threatening. If we put our faith and trust in God and follow him in obedience, this joy will be our joy, and this contentment will be our contentment, and this confidence will be our confidence.

7. Seventh, God does this work in the Christian at the deepest level of their innermost being. This is not a superficial work that God does on the façade of your life. Down in the very depths of your being, this is where God enables you by the strength of the Lord Jesus Christ to do what God would have you do, and it is a comprehensive work that he does. It involves your mind, your affections, and your will.

Imagine being able to write what Paul can write and that it is close to the truth in your own life. Imagine being able to say, *I am content no matter what my circumstances are. I can get along with little, and I know how to live with much. I am content whether I am full or hungry, wealthy or in great need. I can do all things through my Lord, who strengthens me.* Imagine being able to live like this. We can. We have all we need in Christ. Motyer sums it up this way:

> "No circumstance could ever arise which would be too much for Paul's God, and therefore no circumstance could ever beat Paul." (*The Message of Philippians,* page 219)

Paul's God is our God. So when we lack the contentment that Paul enjoyed and exemplified, it is not because we do not have what we need to enjoy it; it is because our eyes are on the wrong place. They are upon our circumstances instead of upon our Savior.

Do you need to be living above your circumstances or are you pulled down in a whirlpool of emotional collapse? Do you need to experience joy in the midst of your situation right now? Do you need to know what it is to say, "I can do all things through [Christ] who strengthens me"? If so, then remember that all joy for your soul and all power for your life is found in the Lord Jesus Christ, and you need to get as close to Christ as you can.

If you will look to him, trust him, live for him, worship him, adore him, serve him, follow him and obey him, then this joy will increase by filling and flooding your soul. I need this; you need this; we all need this. You are either in a very difficult set of circumstances right now, or you are about to head into one, or you have just stepped out of one momentarily to head back into one again. God had only one Son without sin, but he has no sons without sorrow. You will know what it is to be hungry. You may know what it is to be full. But this is the secret which Paul has let us know: you have all you can ever need in Christ, and you can do all things through Christ, who strengthens you.

Questions for reflection

1. What is the secret of contentment? In what ways have you already learned this? In what ways do you still need to learn this?

2. Do you think it is harder to find contentment in Christ when times are hard, or when times are good? Why?

3. How does the final sentence of the last paragraph speak to your soul today?

15. GRATITUDE, GLORY, AND GRACE

As Paul comes to the end of this letter, we do not see a defeated man. Neither do we see one who is discouraged or downcast. Though imprisoned and held in chains, the apostle remains robust in faith and resolute in hope. He is not exasperated with the turn of events that have confined him in Rome for two long years. To the contrary, he is upbeat and triumphant, exuberant in his confidence that God is using him amid this difficulty to spread the gospel to the Roman Empire. Despite his physical hardships and unjust sufferings, he is giving praise to God. Though the outlook was dim, the uplook was never brighter.

In this closing section, Paul concludes with an expression of gratitude for the ministry partnership that he continues to maintain and enjoy with the Philippian Christians. He states his thankfulness for their financial help during these trying times. Finally he ends with a **doxology** of praise for God and final greetings to the believers in Philippi.

Like Paul, you may find yourself in a difficult place in your life. You too may be in a confining set of circumstances from which there is no apparent or immediate escape. If so, take heart as you consider these words of the apostle Paul. His vibrant testimony can be your experience. And if you are not in a trial at the moment, then learn from him, for it is certain that you will find yourself in a trial or hardship at some point. When difficulty comes, make sure that his joy is yours too.

Partnership in Gospel Business

Paul begins this closing section of his epistle by communicating his deep gratitude to the Philippians for the partnership they share together in ministry in which they support him in his ministry: "You have done well to share with me in my affliction" (**v 14**). "Share" (*sungkoinoueo*) means to be a partner together with others. The root word (*koinoueo*) is used elsewhere to mean "have fellowship with, be made a partner." Fellowship means to share something in common with another person in a partnership. The idea is to be a participant with others in a common enterprise. By sending a financial gift, the Philippians were close partners with Paul in the gospel ministry.

This ministry partnership between the Philippians and Paul has been a long-term relationship over many years. He writes, "You yourselves also know, Philippians, that at the first preaching of the gospel, after I left Macedonia, no church shared with me in the matter of giving and receiving but you alone" (**v 15**). "Shared" is, once again, *koinoneo,* the word used for fellowship or partnership. The Philippians had established an ongoing partnership with him beyond that which any other church had known. No church had stood with him for as long as they had. Paul had first preached the gospel in Philippi a decade earlier, and as he then departed for Macedonia, this church remained his ministry partner for a period of ten years. Only the Philippian church had consistently given Paul the financial support he needed to continue his itinerate preaching ministry. As soon as he left Philippi after planting the church there, they immediately began giving financially to meet his needs.

In **verse 15**, Paul uses three business terms. "Giving" refers to expenditures, "receiving" to receipts, and "matter" could be translated "account." These words do not indicate a crass approach to ministry, but the recognition that the Philippians are investing wisely by giving financially to the work of the Lord. Their monetary support of him has been recorded in heaven and it is already yielding an eternal rate of return for God.

Paul remembers that "even in Thessalonica you sent a gift more than once for my needs" (**v 16**). After he left Philippi (Acts 16:40), he had journeyed through Amphipolis and Appollonia until he came to Thessalonica (Acts 17:1). There Paul had preached the gospel and created an uproar, much like the one that had occurred in Philippi. The aftermath of that event was that a church was planted. At a demanding time, when Paul needed financial assistance, the Philippians stood with him with repeated gifts of support. In this sense, they were close partners with him in the work of the gospel.

Making a Profit

The apostle next expresses a disclaimer: that what he desires is not the Philippians' gift, but rather the spiritual reward that is accruing for them: "the profit which increases to your account" (Philippians **4:17**). Whenever someone invests in a business venture, they are allowed to share in the profits earned. By way of metaphor, this is how the financial support of the Philippians is profiting them. By their monetary gifts, the Philippians are storing up an eternal profit for themselves in heaven. Jesus had taught the same: "But store up for yourselves treasures in heaven, where neither moth nor rust destroys, and where thieves do not break in or steal" (Matthew 6:20). In like manner, eternal dividends are being posted to the Philippians' account in heaven.

And this is what matters to Paul, as MacArthur points out:

"Their gift brought Paul joy not because of its personal material benefit to him, but because of its spiritual benefit to them."
(*The MacArthur New Testament Commentary on Philippians,* page 307)

Every believer should be one who invests financially in the work of the Lord. We should be like the Philippians, shrewdly supporting those servants and ministries who are faithfully proclaiming the gospel of Jesus Christ. When we give to the work of spreading the gospel, we are wisely using what has been entrusted to us for the greater glory of God.

Your Money, God's Pleasure, God's Promise

It is not only Paul and the Philippian church that this gift has positively affected. Ultimately, it has brought pleasure to God himself. The apostle has "received from Epaphroditus what you have sent, a fragrant aroma, an acceptable sacrifice, well-pleasing to God" (Philippians **4:18**). He has "received everything in full." That is to say, his needs have been amply supplied. In fact, he has an "abundance" of all that he needs. These generous gifts have been brought to him in Rome by the faithful servant Epaphroditus.

But Paul's main concern is to express that their financial giving to his work serves a much higher purpose than simply meeting his needs. Their stewardship is an act of worship that is being given to God. The apostle uses the imagery of an Old Testament sacrifice being offered by the priest on the altar, which we understand was a sacrifice being given to God. In this act, incense was poured onto the sacrifice, releasing a fragrant aroma that ascended upward to heaven. The sweet-smelling fragrance pictured the pleasure that such a sacrifice brought to God. In like manner, the giving of the Philippian Christians is an expression of their worship of God that is well-pleasing to him.

> Here is the ultimate purpose and the greatest motive for our financial giving.

Here is the ultimate purpose and the greatest motive for our financial giving to gospel ministry. More than meeting the needs of God's ministers, the highest aim is the pleasure it brings to the Father. Such sacrificial gifts are offered as an act of worship that brings pleasure to God. When you realize that your financial support of God's servants is a fragrant sacrifice that brings great pleasure to God, you will find you are a sacrificial giver who can be classified as what Paul called a "cheerful giver" (2 Corinthians 9:7).

Because of their sacrificial giving, Paul announced to the Philippians that God would "supply all your needs according to His riches in glory in Christ Jesus" (Philippians **4:19**). This comes in the form of a promise. Not only would the Philippians receive spiritual blessings in heaven for their giving; but God would also supply many of their physical needs in this life. This generosity from God would come "according to" his riches. There is a vast difference between God merely giving them *out of* his riches and, more correctly, *according to* them. His giving would be in proportion to his vast resources.

This is an important promise that Paul states here. It is true both individually and collectively. As believers give to support those serving in gospel ministry, God will give to these sacrificial givers. Jesus taught the same general principle: "Give, and it will be given to you. They will pour into your lap a good measure—pressed down, shaken together, and running over. For by your standard of measure it will be measured to you in return" (Luke 6:38). Likewise, in churches that give to those ministers who are preaching the word abroad, especially where the name of Christ is not known, God will give to those congregations.

Reasons for Praise

Paul concludes this paragraph by giving glory to God. He exults, "Now to our God and Father be the glory forever and ever. Amen" (Philippians **4:20**). This high doxology is a fitting response to the high theology he has taught in the previous verses:

> "It is no wonder that Paul now concludes the preceding sentence with doxology." (Fee, *Philippians,* page 455)

Because God has so faithfully supplied Paul's needs and promises to provide for the Philippians, the apostle has great reason to offer praise to him. Though Paul finds himself in a difficult situation, he nevertheless abounds in giving glory to God for his goodness toward this supporting church.

Moreover, this verse serves as a concluding doxology in response to all that Paul has written in this letter. Throughout the course of this epistle, Paul has taught the extraordinary truths of the saving grace of God. Each chapter has been packed with triumphant teaching that has magnified the greatness of God, including his grace that is persevering (1:6, 10), faith-granting (1:29), sanctifying (2:13), justifying (3:9), empowering (3:10), glorifying (3:21), and comforting (4:5). The God of such abounding grace must be ascribed the glory due to his name.

Specifically, the first person of the Godhead is to be praised: "our God and Father" is in view (**4:20**). Why should glory be given to the Father? Because he is the Giver of grace (1:2), the Worker of salvation (1:6), the Exalter of Christ (2:9-11), the Conformer of Christ-likeness (2:13), the Father of believers (2:15), the Revealer of truth (3:15), the Giver of peace (4:7, 9), and the Supplier of needs (**4:19**). Consequently, the Father is worthy of praise "forever and ever" (**v 20**). Giving glory to God will be our eternal occupation throughout the ages to come. We should likewise make it our primary occupation in this age too. The only proper response to these truths is to join our affirmation to Paul's *Amen*.

Questions for reflection

1. How has the whole letter to the Philippians shown us what "gospel partnership" is?

2. In what sense does giving money away profit the giver?

3. How have these verses encouraged you to view your money in the way that the Philippian church did? What will taking such a view mean for you practically?

PART TWO

Deep Love, Wide Focus

At the last, Paul comes to the final greetings to be extended from him and the believers in Rome to the believers in Philippi. This is a warm expression of his affection for the saints in both locations. The first greeting is from Paul to the Philippians: "Greet every saint in Christ Jesus" (**v 21**). Paul means to express his love for all the believers in Philippi.

When Paul writes, "Greet every saint," he means far more than merely saying hello on his behalf. The idea conveyed is to communicate the warmth of his affection for the Philippians. He means to extend to them his fervent love for them. As this letter is read, Paul wants them to know his deep love for these brothers and sisters in Christ.

This greeting is extended to "every" saint in Christ Jesus. The word "every" stresses each individual believer in the church. If he had used the word "all," it would have emphasized the church corporately as one large group. But by saying "every," Paul is underscoring how much he individually loves every member in the church.

As discussed earlier, "saint" (*hagios*) is one who has been genuinely regenerated by the Holy Spirit and is set apart from a life of sin unto God to live in holiness. That is what the word "saint" means. Every saint enjoys a fixed, permanent position "in" Christ; every Christian has a vital union with him. Without exception, every believer enjoys communion and fellowship with the Lord Jesus Christ.

Paul serves as a pattern for our Christian lives. We should be openhearted toward one another, showing the love of God to others with whom we share fellowship. Even if we are shy, introverted, and tend to withdraw to ourselves, we must be directed by the Holy Spirit into the lives of other people to greet and embrace them. Equally, if we are independent by nature, we must seek others to love. We must extend warm expressions of the love of God to other believers. Any coldness on the part of a saint was virtually unknown to first-century Christianity. It should be the same in our churches today. We must be affectionate toward one another if we are to advance the gospel. An affectionate Christianity is an effective Christianity.

Greetings from Rome

Paul extends a second greeting in **verse 21**: "The brethren who are with me greet you." This serves to underscore how important greeting other Christians is. Though a prisoner in Rome, Paul was allowed to receive visitors into the house where he was detained. As these people came to Paul, they brought reports of the churches. Paul would write his four prison epistles at this time, to the Ephesians, Philippians, Colossians, and Philemon. Those letters would be taken back to those churches or an individual, expressing greeting from those who were around him.

Paul was sending this greeting with Timothy, who was in prison with him (2:19-24). Epaphroditus was also there (2:25-30). Paul's affectionate love for the Philippians undoubtedly had a stimulating effect upon these men. Other passages indicate that Tychicus, who was the bearer of the letters of Ephesians and Colossians (Colossians 4:7), was with Paul. Philemon may well have been there also. Onesimus—the runaway slave who was the subject of Paul's letter to Philemon—was also there (Colossians 4:9), as was Aristarchus, another longtime companion of the apostle and Mark, who wrote the Gospel of Mark, (Colossians 4:10). In addition, Paul was joined by a man named Jesus (Colossians 4:11), and Luke, who wrote the Gospel of Luke (Colossians 4:14). That is as many as eight people who were with the apostle in his imprisonment. Whether they were all there at one time, we do not know, but Paul expresses greeting from those who are with him.

There is a solidarity in each of their hearts toward the Philippians. They want to be included in this greeting. As Paul writes this final greeting with his own hand, we can imagine that he is looking around the room, and these other men are affirmatively nodding their heads. There may even be some emotion in their voices as they salute the Philippians. This is a house of towering theology, and at the very same time it is a circle of tender love in Christ. It is because of the overflow of their positive fellowship with one another that they make this expression of love to this far-distant church that is so close to their hearts.

As Paul writes his third greeting, the circle is expanding from Paul, to the eight men who are around him, to believers who are in Rome. They, too, express their greeting through this letter of Paul's. The apostle continues, "All the saints greet you" (Philippians **4:22**). The reference is to the believers in Rome, some of whom have had personal contact with him in his house arrest. Paul, speaking on their behalf, communicates their greetings.

"Whether or not they knew that Paul was speaking on their behalf, they are included in Paul's warm exchange of greetings. Paul builds bridges between communities of faith."

(Hansen, *The Letter to the Philippians*, page 331)

What a wonderful unity of Christian love and fellowship this is.

Who are all of these saints in Rome? In Romans 16, we can note who some of these saints are. What is amazing is the fact that as Paul wrote Romans, he had never been to Rome. It would be one thing if he knew all these names after having been there. But he had not traveled there at the time he wrote the letter to the saints in Rome. This testifies how much Paul was attuned to individual people. Paul had never met the people in Romans 16, but it was as though he had lived and pastored in Rome itself.

Paul wrote the letter to the Romans some three to four years before he wrote the letter to the Philippians. Its recipients were people in Rome who were already converted to Christ before Paul later arrived in his imprisonment. This is an indication of how in touch Paul was with the individual churches in Europe and Asia Minor. Paul not only kept up with the problems of those churches, but with the individual people within them. He devoted an entire chapter in his most theological treatise, the book of Romans, to cataloging the names of these people and extending greetings to them.

Three to four years later Paul arrived in Rome as a prisoner, and likely would have met those he had written to and named. It is reasonable to assume that those names mentioned in Romans 16 are included among these saints who are expressing their love to the believers in Philippi.

The King's People in the Emperor's House

A fourth and final greeting is extended from "especially those of Caesar's household" (Philippians **4:22**). This is a highly unlikely group of people who have converted to Christ—those who serve in Caesar's household. Even in the inner recesses of the empire, the word of God is continuing to advance.

These were men and women who served Caesar in the royal palace in Rome. This represented a significant number of people that extended beyond Caesar's own family—including slaves, cooks, food-tasters, musicians, custodians, builders, stablemen, accountants, soldiers, guards, judges, messengers, and heralds. It was a large contingent that found themselves in close proximity to Caesar. They served his needs and kept up with his business. Many of these workers had come to faith in Christ. Paul led some of the praetorian guards—assigned to guard him in this imprisonment—to Christ; they, in turn, carried the gospel back into the palace. This is no doubt intended to be an encouragement to the church in Philippi. There are the saints in Caesar's household who send their greetings. This shows the power of the gospel to reach into the Roman Empire, even into Caesar's own palace. This explosive power is still inherent in the gospel even today.

These new believers in Caesar's household are trophies of God's saving grace. They are in Caesar's household, and yet they are a part of a much larger household, the household of faith. They serve in Caesar's palace but yet they have access to a much greater throne above. They are in Rome, but they have brothers and sisters in Christ all over the known world. No doubt they have heard about the Philippians through their contact with Paul, and they must have urged Paul to communicate to the Philippians their greetings. They are in this together with the rest of the body of Christ. This is what we are to take from **verses 21-22**. These verses are not incidental but a reminder that whoever and wherever we are, if we are "in Christ Jesus," we

> You may travel far from your earthly family, but you are never far from your heavenly family.

are in the family of God together. You may travel anywhere in this world, far away from your earthly family, but you are never far from your heavenly family.

All of Grace

Paul now concludes his letter with this request to God on their behalf: "The grace of the Lord Jesus Christ be with your spirit" (**v 23**). With this, as MacArthur points out:

> "Paul has now come full circle. He began this letter by wishing
> the Philippians grace (1:2), and he concludes it the same way."
> (*The MacArthur New Testament Commentary*
> *on Philippians,* page 318)

"Grace" (*karis*) is unmerited, undeserved favor in the lives of God's people. It is the wellspring and the heartbeat of the Christian life. The believers in Philippi had already received saving grace at the time of their regeneration. Paul nevertheless desires that they know more of this sanctifying grace in their Christian walk, which will enable them to live in a manner that glorifies God, and to do so with joy. This work of preserving grace will continue into eternity future in their glorification. Paul wants them to experience it more fully in their spirits in this life.

This marvelous, joy-filled, Christ-exalting letter now ends as it began, with an emphasis upon the grace of God being even more fully bestowed upon his people (1:2). From the new birth to the new heavens and new earth, the Christian life is entirely one of grace. Start to finish, it is *all* of grace. Rejoice!

Questions for reflection

1. How has the whole letter of the Philippians shown you what it looks like to be an open-hearted church? How are you adopting this approach to your own church family?

2. What does a true belief in the power of the gospel do to our proclamation of that gospel?

3. If you had to sum up the message of Philippians in a single sentence, what would you say?

GLOSSARY

Active voice: grammatical term. In the active voice, the main subject of the sentence is acting, e.g. "The man [subject] ate [active verb] two hamburgers". In the passive voice, the subject of the sentence is acted upon, e.g. "Two hamburgers [the subject] were eaten [passive verb] by the man". Somewhere in between is the **middle voice**—this occurs in Greek but there is no direct equivalent in modern English. In Greek it implies that the subject acts on itself, e.g. "The girl [the subject] washes [i.e. she washes herself]".

Affirmative: agreeing with a statement.

Alumni: the former students of a school or college.

Antithesis: the direct opposite.

Apostle: a man appointed by the risen Christ to teach about him with authority.

AWOL: to be absent from where one is supposed to be (from the military acronym of Absent Without Official Leave).

Benediction: blessing.

Blasé: indifferent to or casual with something because it is so familiar.

Brethren: brothers and sisters; the church family.

Chastisement: discipline.

Common grace: good things which God gives regardless of whether someone is a Christian or not (e.g. rain, air).

Corollary: the next step logically; something which must be true if the statement before is true.

Deity: divine status; being fully God.

Doctrine: the study of what is true about God; or a statement about an aspect of that truth. To be **doctrinally sound** is to believe and express correct doctrine.

Downgrade Controversy: a controversy (1887-1888) that led to Charles Spurgeon's church, the Metropolitan Tabernacle in London, leaving the Baptist Union. Spurgeon accused other Baptists of having "downgraded" their view of the Bible, and consequently falling into doctrinal error: denying the deity of Christ, the atonement, etc.

Doxology: a hymn or liturgy of praise to God.

Edification: instruction, education, building up.

Epistle: letter.

Epitome: the perfect example of a certain quality.

Evangelist: someone who equips other Christians to tell non-Christians the gospel of Jesus Christ, and who is gifted at doing this themselves.

Fallen: affected by God's judgment, which was a consequence of the fall—the event when the first man and woman disobeyed God (see Genesis 3).

Glorification: the moment when one of God's people is made perfect, like Christ, and welcomed into God's eternal kingdom.

Godhead: the one God is three Persons, distinct from one another, each fully God, of the same "essence" (or "God-ness"). These three Persons—the Father, the Son and the Holy Spirit—make up the Godhead.

Gospel: The proclamation that the man Jesus was also God himself, came to serve us and to rule us as our King; that he died for sins; that he rose to rule and give new life; that he is reigning in heaven and will return to restore the world. The gospel is good news to be believed, not good advice to be followed.

Grace: undeserved, overflowing generosity. In the Bible, "grace" is usually used to describe how God treats his people. Because God is full of grace, he gives believers eternal life (see Ephesians 2:4-8) and all the current blessings that flow from relationship with him; he also gives them gifts to use to serve his people (see Ephesians 4:7, 11-13) and to continue in faith.

Heresy: wrong teaching that goes against accepted Christian belief.

Indulgences: in Roman Catholicism, a reduction of the amount of time a soul has to spend being punished in purgatory after death. An indulgence, it is thought, can be acquired by saying a special prayer, donating money to the church, performing a particular deed, etc.

Itinerant: traveling from place to place.

Judaizers: a group in the early church who taught that Christians must also keep the Jewish law and customs, such as circumcision, in order to be saved.

Last rites: the rituals a Roman Catholic or Orthodox priest conducts with a dying person, which includes various prayers and taking communion.

Means of grace: the things (or "means") by which Christians grow spiritually and experience God's blessing.

Meekness: humility, gentleness.

Metaphorically: a metaphor is where one thing is a symbol for a deeper truth.

Middle voice: see definition for **active voice**.

Ministry: the work of proclaiming the gospel to people (both Christians and non-believers).

Mosaic law: the Old Testament laws, which God gave Moses in the books of Exodus, Leviticus, Numbers and Deuteronomy, and which lay out how Israel is to relate to God and live as his people.

Motif: recurring idea or pattern.

Mutually inclusive: occurring at the same time (as opposed to mutually _exclusive_, when if you have one you cannot have the other).

New birth: the moment when someone becomes a Christian and becomes a child of God. Jesus said that everyone must be "born again" of the Spirit (John 3:1-8)—before this moment we are dead in our sins (Ephesians 2:1).

Objective: a truth or status which is based on facts, not feelings, e.g. "I am married to this woman." For comparison see **subjective**.

Paradox: two true statements that seem to be contradictory, but are not.

Positionally: referring to our position before God.

Praetorian guard: the Roman emperor's personal bodyguards.

Prefix: grammatical term. An element added to the front of a word which affects its meaning. E.g. "unhurt"—"un" is the prefix.

Prepositional: a preposition is a word or phrase used to connect two nouns, which affects the meaning of a sentence. E.g. "The mouse under [preposition] the box," "The mouse near [preposition] the box."

Prerogatives: rights or privileges.

Present tense: grammatical term, denoting that something is happening or is true now. E.g. "I worked in New York" (past tense); "I work in New York" (present tense).

Protagonists: a leading character in a text or story; in this case, the Philippian Christians.

Providentially: describing something that has happened as part of God's plan, under his protective care and power.

Puritan: a member of a sixteenth- and seventeenth-century movement in Great Britain which was committed to the Bible as God's word, to simpler worship services, to greater commitment and devotion to following Christ, and increasingly to resisting the institutional church's hierarchical structures. Many emigrated to what would become the US, and were a strong influence on the church in many early colonies.

Quietist: an approach which grew popular in the 1670s and 1680s—it promoted the idea that we grow closest to God through rest, inaction and a withdrawn, quiet contemplation.

Rebirth: see definition for **new birth**.

Reciprocal: doing something in return.

Redeemer: Jesus Christ, the one who redeemed (freed, released, bought back for a price) his people.

Regenerating: describes God giving new, spiritual life. See also the definition for **new birth**.

Sanctification: the process of someone growing in purity and Christ-likeness (see Romans 8:29).

Second person: writing using the pronouns "you/yours," as opposed to "I/mine" (first person) or "him/her/his/hers" (third person).

Stoic: enduring pain without complaining.

Subjective: something which is based on feelings and opinions. E.g. "She is the most beautiful woman in the world" is a subjective opinion. For comparison see **objective**.

Substitutionary: an act that involves a replacement, where someone (or something) stands in or is substituted for another.

Synonym: a word that has the same meaning as another.

Tarry: delay.

Tenet: a principle or belief.

Theologian: someone who studies theology—the study of the truth about God.

BIBLIOGRAPHY

- James Montgomery Boice, *Philippians* in the Expositional Commentary series (Baker, 2000)

- Thomas Brooks, *Heaven on Earth: A Treatise on Christian Assurance* (Banner of Truth, 1961)

- John Calvin, *The Epistles of Paul the Apostle to the Galatians, Ephesians, Philippians and Colossians* (Eerdmans, 1996)

- Gordon Fee, *Paul's Letter to the Philippians* in the New International Commentary on the New Testament series (Eerdmans, 1995)

- G. Walter Hansen, *The Letter to the Philippians* in the Pillar New Testament Commentary series (Eerdmans, 2009)

- William Hendriksen, *Philippians* in the New Testament Commentary series (Baker, 1962)

- Dennis E. Johnson, *Philippians* in the Reformed Expository Commentary series (P&R, 2013)

- D. Martyn Lloyd-Jones, *The Assurance of Our Salvation (Studies in John 17)* (Crossway, 2000)

- John MacArthur, *The MacArthur New Testament Commentary on Philippians* (Moody, 2001)

- J. Alec Motyer, *The Message of Philippians* in The Bible Speaks Today series (IVP UK, 1984)

- Richard Sibbes, *The Works of Richard Sibbes* ed. Alexander B. Grosart (Banner of Truth, 1983)

- John Stott, *Basic Christianity* (IVP USA, 2006)

- Benjamin B. Warfield, "Predestination" *in Biblical Doctrines* (Baker, 1932)

- George Whitfield, *Sermons of George Whitfield* (Hendrickson, 2009)

Philippians for...
Bible-study Groups

Steven Lawson's **Good Book Guide** to Philippians is the companion to this resource, helping groups of Christians to explore, discuss and apply the book together. Seven studies—each including investigation, apply, getting personal, pray, and explore more sections—take you through the whole book. Includes a concise Leader's Guide at the back.

the Good Book Guide to **Philippians**

Philippians
Shining with joy

7 studies   by Steven J Lawson

Find out more at:
www.thegoodbook.com/goodbookguides

Daily Devotionals

Explore daily devotional helps you open up the Scriptures and will encourage and equip you in your walk with God. Published as a quarterly booklet, *Explore* is also available as an app, where you can download Dr Lawson's notes on Philippians, alongside contributions from trusted Bible teachers including Albert Mohler, Timothy Keller, Mark Dever, David Helm, and Sam Allberry.

Find out more at:
www.thegoodbook.com/explore

thegoodbook
COMPANY

BIBLICAL | RELEVANT | ACCESSIBLE

At The Good Book Company, we are dedicated to helping Christians and local churches grow. We believe that God's growth process always starts with hearing clearly what he has said to us through his timeless word—the Bible.

Ever since we opened our doors in 1991, we have been striving to produce resources that honour God in the way the Bible is used. We have grown to become an international provider of user-friendly resources to the Christian community, with believers of all backgrounds and denominations using our Bible studies, books, evangelistic resources, DVD-based courses and training events.

We want to equip ordinary Christians to live for Christ day by day, and churches to grow in their knowledge of God, their love for one another, and the effectiveness of their outreach.

Call us for a discussion of your needs or visit one of our local websites for more information on the resources and services we provide.

Your friends at The Good Book Company

NORTH AMERICA
UK & EUROPE
AUSTRALIA
NEW ZEALAND

thegoodbook.com
thegoodbook.co.uk
thegoodbook.com.au
thegoodbook.co.nz

866 244 2165
0333 123 0880
(02) 9564 3555

WWW.CHRISTIANITYEXPLORED.ORG
Our partner site is a great place for those exploring the Christian faith, with a clear explanation of the good news, powerful testimonies and answers to difficult questions.